Someone To Love Me

By

Connie Joy Sharp

authorHOUSE™

1663 LIBERTY DRIVE, SUITE 200
BLOOMINGTON, INDIANA 47403
(800) 839-8640
WWW.AUTHORHOUSE.COM

First published by AuthorHouse 11/30/05

ISBN: 1-4208-8846-3 (sc)

Printed in the United States of America
Bloomington, Indiana

This book is printed on acid-free paper.

A true, personal story of domestic violence, substance abuse and triumph.

Table of Contents

Prologue

There was a time (not so long ago) when I honestly believed my story was unique, and that it should be kept buried like an ugly secret. Now, I know better.

Now, I know that I am just one of the millions of women in our Country who live with the effects of domestic violence and abuse. Now I know that the shame and fear attached to "being discovered" can trap its victims in a formidable web of pain and sickening dependency.

If you are a victim of abuse, you know what it's like to live with constant confusion, and a sourceless guilt that offers no hope for escape. My sincere prayer is that you will see in this book of memories a mirror of your own painful experiences, your own desperate fears, and the route to your own salvation.

It's only because of God's love for me that I can even begin to tell this story. He gives me courage and He wipes away my tears as I remember things I would much rather forget and keep hidden in the past.

I dedicate this effort and its use to my Lord, Jesus Christ. He is my Father, my best Friend, my Guide, my Salvation. Jesus Christ waited for me with His arms outstretched to forgive, to love, and to heal.

He waits for you too. Seek and you will find Him.

Connie Sharp

Please Love Me

A Child's Most Earnest Wish

Oh how little children love to be loved! Happy, happy are the little ones who find it.

Sometimes it's funny to watch how far these tiny master manipulators will go to earn those precious warm hugs...soft kisses...and reassuring smiles. But a child's never-ending search for attention, approval, and praise shouldn't be a surprise. After all, it comes from the same deep-seated need inside everyone — to be loved.

Knowing they're loved is what makes little people feel safe. And that security is the best gift a parent or guardian can give. Little ones who are nurtured with a lot of loving support learn to face life with self confidence — a sense of believing they deserve whatever good comes their way and the ambition to go looking for it.

But what happens to children who grow up without the love and nurture they deserve? What does their future promise?

The search for love goes on and on.

Life can be a lonely, scary place for a child who feels unwanted... unloved...abandoned. It's there that first impressions of self-worth — or the *lack* of it — are tragically and indelibly written in stone. It's a place where souls are branded with a deep and indescribable longing that will burn for many, many years to come.

I know this to be true. I was there.

....

My life began on January 1, 1939, in Marshall, a small town in south central Michigan. The occasion couldn't be called a "blessed event" by any stretch of the imagination.

The truth is, my entry into the world was a pretty silly scenario — with no purpose at all! The whole thing was so obviously pointless, there were many times when I wondered why the mysterious controller of things like life and death allowed me to be born at all.

From the time I can remember having any sort of real impression about "things," I knew that *I* was the unfortunate by-product of a devious (and admittedly regrettable) trick that my Mother played on my Father.

I'll never quite understand how the term "fooled into it" applies to conception — the facts of life seem pretty self-explanatory to me! But, be that as it may, the story I was told goes something like this...

While my Father wasn't looking, My Mother "fooled" him right into having a baby! She knew he didn't want a child, so she kept her efforts to conceive a secret. And, then, she concealed her pregnancy somehow until it was too late to comply with my Father's pleas for an immediate abortion.

It shouldn't have worked. But it did.

In retrospect, there was never any shame over the whole affair. Nor was there any attempt to deny it.

Mother bluntly described my worth by saying, "If it wasn't for me saving your unborn hide, you never would have been born. Your Father never wanted you."

In my Mother's defense, I know she loved me in her own way. And, now, I realize that she did her best to prove it. But she couldn't make up for the total apathy that came from my Father.

From him there was no love. There was no hate either. He simply ignored me. My Father seemed completely oblivious to the fact that I existed. I felt invisible...not even important enough to be a nuisance!

My Father's self-imposed distance and his complete lack of affection made me feel as though there was something about me that was unlovable. I had the distinct sense that his rejection was somehow *my* fault.

I remember wondering if I would ever be good enough...if I would ever find *someone to love me.*

terror in the night

Still today, thinking about my earliest memories, a terror fills my chest. A scream freezes in my throat just like it did when I was only three years old.

When I lie still and listen, I remember the rats — what sounds like thousands of tiny clawed feet running up and down inside the wall next to me. I can feel myself burrowing deeper under the blankets in my crib in the dark, cold, little room and listening to those awful, telltale sounds.

Sometimes the nasty rodents found a way out of the wall and ran around the floor. I used to hold my breath hoping the rats wouldn't run up the sides of my crib and find me. Then when terror overcame, I'd cry out for someone to come and save me.

I don't know what my Father hated more — the sounds of my screams or rats in the house. But when he got fed up with the noise, he'd come in my room...catch one of the little varmints... and then stab it with a knife until it died.

One especially horrible night, I awoke in a scramble of wet, bloody blankets. A rat had been biting me and was still sitting on my arm nibbling right through my skin. I don't remember it hurting so much. I only remember the sheer terror of being invaded.

I screamed and screamed for what seemed like forever before my Mother came to help. Daddy wasn't far behind with his knife. I can still feel my ears sting when I recall how hard I covered them with my hands so I wouldn't hear the awful death ritual.

There was never any concern for me or attempt to calm the fears that pervaded each night.

for a father's love

My Father didn't spend his time with me. I don't recall any hugs or kisses. I never heard him say, "I love you."

Even today, so many years later, I can still feel the terrific longing. I wanted so very badly to sit on his lap. I can hear my silent begging.

Daddy, please tell me you love me and kiss me goodnight. Let me sit on your lap. Just hold me, Daddy.
Talk to me, Daddy. Tell me I am your little girl.
Carry me, Daddy. Take me places with you, please.
I love you, Daddy. Won't you love me, too?
Maybe if I am really quiet and good, he'll begin to love me a little. I will just wait, and I won't make any noise. Then maybe he'll come home and kiss me goodnight.

But he never did.

a mother's example

We were one of those families that, for no apparent reason, kept moving to different places — never far away from each other — just different. With every change, I always hoped that a new house would mean a different kind of life. But one place was no different from another.

The most lasting impressions of the places we called 'home' are filled with visions of dark, cold rooms and the fright of pure lonliness.

6

When I was three years old, my Mother gave birth to another baby girl. Her name was Shirley.

Now, I don't know if Shirley was a "trick" too, or if her birth was actually planned. But no matter the case, my Father reacted in the same way. Neither of us was even the smallest part of his concerns.

My parents didn't spend much affection on each other either. Unless they were yelling at one another — which was almost all the time — they acted more like strangers than family.

When I was six years old, my Father bought a used car lot. To save on expenses, we rented an old house that doubled as a business office for the car sales lot.

It was cramped and dirty and ugly. Old cars were parked haphazardly all around the house. There wasn't a yard — only black cinders scattered around — and that's where my sister and I played.

My Father was gone a lot of the time...gambling I've heard. We saw him during the day, out in the car lot, talking to customers. But then at night he disappeared until the next morning.

One early morning, instead of seeing my Father, I saw a man I didn't know coming out of my parents' room. My Mom was walking beside him with her arm around his waist. They seemed so happy. They were giggling and kissing each other in a way I'd never before seen adults act.

After that first surprise encounter, I guess my Mother figured she didn't need to hide her nighttime visitors from Shirley and me anymore. The news was out. And that same man became a regular visitor at our house whenever my Father was gone.

At first I didn't mind too much because he made my Mother happier than I'd ever seen her. But after a while, things started to change. He started to act strangely. He talked too loudly and seemed anxious about every little thing. It wasn't long before he was screaming at my Mother all of the time — just like my Father did.

Once, after my Mother told him not to come over anymore, he got very drunk and snuck into our house through a window. I don't know what he wanted to do, but my Mother said, "Connie, take Shirley and hide. Quickly! And don't come out until I come and get you."

I grabbed Shirley's hand. We picked the nearest closet and slammed the door shut. We scrunched together and huddled as far back into the tiny space as we could — until we were practically stifled by hanging clothes and darkness.

We were so frightened. We swallowed our cries and tears so no one would hear us. And we squeezed each other hard to keep each other from shaking. We couldn't hear a thing — just a terrible, deafening silence.

After a long time, Shirley and I heard heavy foot steps in the hallway — he was half running, half staggering in our direction. We heard him calling my mother's name. We froze.

Suddenly he grabbed the closet door handle and yanked it open. Shirley and I flattened ourselves on the floor in that dark, little cavern under all the hanging clothes.

We were certain he would find us. And he probably would have if he hadn't heard, at that exact moment, voices coming from downstairs. As quickly as he opened the door, he slammed it shut and the blackness became our cover again.

We waited and waited for Mother to come and rescue us — all the while straining to hear someone or something familiar. Finally I decided to look. I crawled to the door and pushed it very slowly and carefully until there was crack just big enough to see through.

There was no one there. The hall was empty. The bad man was gone!

Shirley and I crawled out of the closet, our hearts pounding, and ran down the hall to our bedroom. We locked the door behind us and ran straight for the window.

Outside, we saw a police officer talking to Mother at the end of our driveway. Our most feared assailant slumped in the back of the police car.

Shirley and I just stood there looking out the window trying to figure out what was happening. We were so little. And this was too confusing.

In our alarmed, childish way we kept asking each other, "Why did my Mom let the bad man come to our house? How come she's not happy when he comes over anymore? Where is Daddy? Doesn't he want us?"

It was impossible for us to understand these happenings way back then. And my Mother didn't try to explain.

She refused to answer our questions. But she saw our fear and did her best to reassure us that the scary, bad man would never be back.

And that's one promise she kept. We never saw him again.

But there were other men — so many that I eventually failed to be surprised by the strangers coming and going from our house. My Mother never quit trying.

She was looking for *someone to love her.*

My Mom was one of nine children. When she was just three years old, her Father died of alcoholism. It was a horrible loss because, after his death, my grandmother had no means of supporting her children.

To protect then from the despair of poverty, hunger, and hopelessness, my grandmother did the most difficult thing any Mother could do. She took my Mother and her eight brothers and sisters to a catholic orphanage.

The group was met at the train by sisters from the orphanage. One-by-one, my grandmother said goodbye to her precious children. As my grandmother tried to pass my Mother to one of the sisters, my Mother would not let go of my grandmother's hand.

She was crying and pleading, "Mommy, mommy, please don't leave me." But, Grandmother had no choice but to pull her hand away and leave everything in the world she loved.

My Mother told us that she cried for days in her unfriendly, new home. It felt like a prison. The orphanage was cold and dark. The sisters were very strict with their little wards.

The children were often hungry. But if they complained they were spanked. Discipline was the substitute for a mother's love. My Mother and her brothers and sisters had a terrible childhood — void of the love they hungered for and needed. They felt deserted.

My Mother was a teenager before my grandmother could bring her children back to live with her. She spent her most formative childhood years in a lonely, frightening place. She never knew love growing up, and her hunger for it never ended.

My Mother was 16 when she met my Father. He was 32. She remembers being warned about the potential dangers of such a relationship, but this first taste of love was so overwhelming, my sixteen-year-old Mother wouldn't listen to any advice. She ran away from home and got married to the first person who promised to care for her.

I often wondered why she thought my Father loved her. Maybe he acted like he did then. Maybe they were happy when they were first together. I don't know. All I remember is my Father yelling at her, and her yelling back.

if only he would die

Their relationship deteriorated to a place beyond rotten. I remember my Mother saying over and over again to Shirley and me, "Pray that your Father will go away. Pray that hell just die."

She went to card readers and told us the reader said that my Father would die soon. That forecast made her so happy. She twirled around and laughed, "Everything will be all right when he's gone."

So, like an obedient little girl, I prayed for our father's demise. We figured, just like our Mother did, that she could replace our sorry excuse for a Father with a man that really loved us.

We prayed and prayed and waited and waited.

But, instead of disappearing, my Father flourished. He was offered another job selling cars in Detroit, and he jumped at the chance. This was his first chance at the "big time."

So, when I was seven years old, off we all went to live a small apartment in the "Old Detroit" district — a section of the city filled with huge, dilapidated old houses.

The new job didn't work out so well for my dad. It wasn't long before his chance at the "big time" turned sour.

He went from one car dealership to another. Of course it was never his fault. He explained, "Oh that place wasn't worth it anyway. No one knows how lucky they are to have me."

There were always dry spells between his jobs when there was no income. My parents struggled and struggled to pay their bills and they argued constantly. They couldn't even manage to pay for the essentials.

Out of necessity, my Mother found a job in a factory. The job solved the money trouble, but instigated another set of problems. Within weeks, she was having an affair with one of her co-workers.

When Shirley and I wondered aloud about what she was doing, Mother told us not to worry. She said, "It's all right for me to go out with other men because your Father doesn't care about us. And he's going to die soon anyway."

foreshadows of a. life to come

I started growing up in more ways than one! I looked more "mature" than my mere 13 years — in fact I looked not a day younger than 18. Older boys and men looked at me with total admiration.

Oh, how I loved the attention! To me, it was proof of their approval, and it felt absolutely wonderful. I had finally found not just one, but a whole lot of men who *loved me.*

When I figured out that I could attract attention, I never quit looking for it. We moved from the apartment into a big old house on the corner of a busy street. It was there that I discovered how much fun it was to get all dressed up and walk up and down the sidewalk from one corner to another.

Men honked their horns and yelled compliments at me as they drove by. I really thought I was something. Men were telling me how desirable I was, and of course, I believed it.

What I didn't realize then was that I was headed for big, big trouble. I was not only content with seeking drive-by approvals, I was ready to equate these cheap expressions with true love.

Just like my Mother, I was searching for *someone to love me.*

first taste of abuse

During summer vacations from school, I went to Ohio and stayed with my Aunt and Uncle for a week. I truly believe that my Mother thought it was a special treat for me to get away from home, and spend some time with my cousins. She had no way of knowing the real story.

In truth, my relatives' home was just as bad, if not worse, than my own. My Uncle was a big, mean, angry man. He was an alcoholic with absolutely no conscience or warmth.

He made me feel very uncomfortable. Maybe it was the sly glances...maybe it was his silence...maybe he was just too ugly. I can't really define the source of my discomfort, but I didn't like to be around him.

He yelled at my Aunt until she simply gave up trying to please him. Instead, she spent her days just trying to stay out of his way.

And then there was Jean, my older cousin by three years. She was big and fat and constantly dirty. She inherited her father's unusually mean spirit plus some! It seemed to me that her goal in life was to make me as miserable as she could. She scared me to death.

During those summertime visits, things happened in that house that I'll never forget. It is a nightmare of abuse that began one horrible night and didn't stop until I finally refused to go back.

The night it all began, Jean and I were talking in the upstairs bedroom we shared during my visits. At first, everything seemed pretty normal. But all of a sudden Jean yanked open a door that I'd not noticed before at the side of the room. It led to the attic above the room.

I was so startled. I remember asking, "What are you doing?"

Jean grabbed me, yanked me across the room, and pushed me through the door into the attic. It was like a pitch black, musty cave. She pulled the door shut and locked it behind me.

I stopped for minute and listened...stunned.

Jean is just trying to scare me. She won't leave me locked in here all by myself.

But I couldn't hear any noises. It was perfectly silent in the bedroom. Jean locked the door and left!

I screamed and screamed until I heard Jean come back into the bedroom. But no matter how hard I begged, she wouldn't open the door. She just kept laughing at me. The louder I cried the harder she laughed.

I don't know how long I was locked in that black abyss — it seemed like an eternity. I do know that I never stopped screaming. And Jean never stopped laughing.

My Aunt must have heard my cries and came to explore. When she came into the bedroom and figured out what was happening, she unlocked the attic door and let me out. But that was the end of her sympathy.

I couldn't stop shaking and crying, but my Aunt and Uncle had no comforting words for me or warnings for Jean. The three of them just kept yelling, "Shut up. Quit your fussing. You're acting like a spoiled brat. You're just a great big sniffling baby."

I was so scared. I wanted to call my Mother but they just snickered as though my request was ridiculous, and refused to let me near the phone.

I felt like a panicky little rabbit with wolves circling. All I wanted to do was get out of that house and as far away as my legs would carry me. But they wouldn't let me leave.

And the nightmare continued.

Later that night, when Jean and I got into the bed we shared, she began to caress my body in foreign, disgusting ways. She held me down with her giant legs and molested me.

It felt terrible. It hurt. It was dirty and shameful.

But I was so frightened of her. She was so big and mean, I didn't know what to do — how to protest. I couldn't make her stop.

And it didn't stop. It went on and on. Jean warned me never to tell or she'd do something terrible to me. And she said, "Do what I tell you, or you'll be sorry, you big baby."

So the shameful activities continued night after night in that horrible dark bedroom — summer after summer. She raped my body and soul until I felt sick.

One especially warm evening, during my last visit to Ohio, I was outside on the porch with my Aunt and cousins. My Aunt asked me to go into the kitchen and get sodas for everyone.

As I walked through the living room, my Uncle, wearing only his boxer shorts was sitting alone in his usual spot — a big leather chair in front of the TV — with a case of beer at his side. I walked behind him as quietly as I could, hoping not to attract his attention.

But I wasn't quiet enough. He turned and looked at me with an ugly, drunken grin and said, "Where are you going, pretty baby?"

I pretended to just ignore him, but he got up and followed me into the kitchen. He walked very slowly, almost creeping, until he was right behind me. I was determined not to turn around and face him, but he was so close I could feel his breath on my hair.

Suddenly, he swung me around and pushed his body hard against me. I was trapped. It was the most terrifying moment of my life — this huge, drunk man kissing me and touching my body with a lascivious freedom.

I yelled at the top of my lungs and tried to push him away. But, Uncle put one hand over my mouth and continued the awful groping with his other hand. He was so strong — so much bigger than I. I couldn't move.

Finally, over Uncle's shoulder, I saw my Aunt standing in the kitchen doorway. I hadn't heard her come in. I don't know how long she had been watching. But she was just staring into space. She didn't appear angry or even surprised.

Deliberately, Aunt walked over to where my Uncle had backed me against the wall, and pulled him away from me. She didn't say a word. And neither did my Uncle. He just laughed like a devil and went back to his chair and his beer.

I didn't know what to do. I was angry, scared, and confused. My Aunt finally broke the silence when she said, "If you tell anyone about this, I'll tell them it was your fault. I'll say you flirted with your Uncle until he couldn't ignore it anymore, you cheap little slut."

I never did tell anyone. And I never went back to their house again.

Love was When

The Search Goes On and On

What becomes of little girls who don't receive the love and reassurance they so desperately need? Many will keep trying to find attention (which they confuse for love) from others — and often in the most unlikely places. It might not be a conscious choice, but most can't stop trying.

They are so eager to find love they'll talk themselves into settling for tiny hints of approval — no matter how meaningless or infrequent. Yet the victims of childhood neglect or abuse may be so conditioned to believe they never will find love that they can actually convince themselves it's their own fault when they don't. A scared child can be heard inside every abused woman who insists: "It was my fault, really. I just seem to provoke him somehow."

The search for love can be a desperate journey that is full of rejection and disappointments. Hopes are dashed. Promises are broken. Dreams go unfulfilled.

There never seems to be an end of counterfeit lovers. The man she thinks is her savior turns into an awful stranger. And she always realizes too late that she's made another terrible mistake.

It's so scary. It seems so unfair.

Love shouldn't be so painful.

I don't know exactly how the experiences of youth affect the way we behave as adults. But when I look at myself and the string of mistakes and poor choices I've made, it isn't hard to see that I was working from a framework created by some pretty unhealthy role models, and a terribly low self esteem factor.

I wanted to be loved so badly. But I really didn't know what loving someone meant. I knew there was a gaping, empty spot inside me that so desperately wanted to belong to someone. But, I knew nothing about mutual esteem between two people, or the comfort of caring smiles, or the security of unconditional affection.

I simply figured that *loving* someone meant having a sexual relationship. So — starting at a very young age — that's exactly what I did. And the only way I knew to begin was to follow my mother's example.

I suppose my first experiment with *loving* was triggered by an adolescent's feeling of loneliness in a new place. When I was 14 years old, my Father was offered another job in East Lansing so we moved again. I had to start ninth grade in a new school, and I hated it. I felt so alone and disconnected.

To bring in extra money, my Mother rented spare rooms to boys who were college students at the nearby State University. It was nice to have people coming and going from the house. It made me feel secure and like part of a real family.

And it was so much fun to flirt with my new friends. But before long, I was doing a whole lot more than flirting. I started sleeping with one of the students. At night, when everyone else was asleep, he came to my bedroom and we tried out every form of sex play the two of us could imagine.

It was such a wonderful feeling. He was mine and I was his. He said he loved me and I believed him. At 14 years old, I never felt the tiniest bit of guilt or shame.

Finally...I found *someone to love me.*

Ken

At 16, I quit school and began babysitting for some of my mother's friends. One afternoon, while I was watching the children, a man came to the house. His name was Ken, and he was a real estate agent who had been called to look over the property and list it for sale.

It was definitely "love at first sight" — at least for me. He was very good looking, and had a really comfortable personality. Instantly, I decided that I would do everything in my power to make him mine.

Ken came to the house three times that week to measure rooms and check things out. At first, he didn't seem too interested in me. He was friendly enough, but not overly attentive.

So I pushed and pushed for more attention. I didn't care that he was 26 years old and I was only 16. I dressed for him...walked for him....smiled for him... and dreamed of him.

Slowly but surely, he began to show signs of interest. He hung around longer than he needed to. And I could tell from the way he looked at me that he was finally noticing my efforts.

Finally, Ken asked me to go out on a date. He played in a dance band, and he took me along. I was simply overwhelmed. He was wonderful. He was popular, handsome, fun, and he *loved me.*

We started spending a lot of time together. We went everywhere together. And we slept together whenever we could.

Ken was the only thing in life that mattered to me. He made me feel special. I wanted to be everything to him. I couldn't think about anything but how to please him. I had to be everything he needed so I would never lose him.

I had this wonderful, secure feeling with Ken. He was always looking out for me. He told me I was his and his alone. He always wanted to know where I was and what I was doing because *he loved me.*

Ken even found a job for me as a receptionist in a doctor's office. It wasn't an easy position for a 17-year old girl. The responsibilities were too much for me. But I wanted so much to please him, I did the very best I could.

Ken came by the office several times a day to check on me. I loved him so much. I dressed the way he wanted. I fixed my hair the way he liked it. I talked the way he suggested. Everything I did, I did to make him happy and proud of me.

And it worked — for a little while, at least. But the job was getting harder and harder for me to do well. My home life was a wild mess of constant fighting. I was tired. And I began to show the stress.

One day, Ken stopped by the office like always. But that day something was very wrong.

He acted like a different person. Instead of his usual smile and caring words, he took one look at me and grumbled, "God, you look terrible! What's gotten into you?"

I was horrified. "What's wrong," I cried, "What do you mean?"

"You look like a messed-up little kid trying to play grown-up," Ken said with a nasty scowl. "For god's sake, shape up, Connie!"

And with that, he was gone.

It was late in the afternoon, and the doctor had gone home for the day. I just sank down in my chair at the desk...put my hands over my face...and cried and cried. I was devastated. Everything that meant anything to me just walked out the door and left me alone.

I felt so tired...so hopeless...so sick of the fight. I had tried my best and I lost.

Without thinking about what I was about to do or the implications, I walked back to the medicine cabinet and unlocked the door. I found a bottle of sleeping pills and very slowly and methodically counted out 20 tablets, put them in my mouth, and swallowed them. Then, I went back to my desk, collected my purse, put my coat on, and left the office.

I don't remember being afraid. I wanted to find my Mother and sink into a deep, everlasting sleep in her arms.

The last thing I recall is walking down the street toward the grocery store where my Mother worked. Then everything went black.

I don't recall hearing the details of what happened next. I don't know how I got from that street into a hospital emergency ward.

But I'll never forget how I felt when I woke. I was engulfed alone in a deep hole that seemed endless, black, and terrifying.

When I was strong enough to go home, the first thing I did was call Ken. I cried for him to come back. I begged for his forgiveness.

Forgiveness for what? It didn't matter to me. I just needed him back in my life. I wanted to please him.

Ken agreed to try again and we picked up our lives like nothing unusual had happened. I was happy and secure again...I had *someone to love me.*

Dick

During the last half of my 17th year, my parents moved again. It was a small house, but in my memory, it was the best house and the happiest place we ever lived.

The home was located in an "upscale" part of town, near a quaint little business section. It made us all feel like we'd finally climbed higher on the social ladder. There was a constant flow of activity, and people were friendly there.

In just a short time, I made new acquaintances — the most memorable of which was the owner of the television store around the corner. His name was Dick, and he was so handsome and mature. I liked him the minute I saw him, and it wasn't hard to see that the feeling was mutual.

When I found out that Dick was a business owner, I asked if he might know of any job openings in the area. I couldn't believe my good fortune when he responded with a smile, saying that in fact, *he* was looking for someone to answer the phones and help customers in *his* store. Dick said, "Stop in the store during the next couple of days, and we can talk about the job. We'll see what happens and go from there."

I thought I would die of excitement. I could hardly wait to go. But I wasn't going *only* to interview for a job. My priority was this handsome man who was showering me with attention and approval.

Somehow or another I managed to wait two days before showing up at Dick's door. And, oh, the preparations involved!

I wanted to be the most beautiful woman he'd ever seen. I got all dressed up to look as old and as appealing as possible. And it worked.

When I walked into that store, everyone turned and looked at me. Dick did too with a knowing, possessive smile of approval. I knew at once that he was "hooked." He was mine. He would *love me*.

I started working the next day.

It didn't matter to me that at 42 years, Dick was more than twice my age, or that he was married with five children. The only thing I cared about was the warm feeling I got when he paid attention to me.

And pay attention he did.

One week into my new job, Dick asked if I could work late.

I said, "Sure, anytime."

So, that same night, after the store closed, Dick and I went into his office. He didn't continue the pretense for even one minute.

Immediately, Dick walked up behind me, turned me around, and kissed me. I felt warm everywhere, and I had chills at the same time. It was overwhelming joy.

Dick fixed a few drinks. We were laughing and touching and kissing. Neither of us had a care in the world. We made love until very late into the night. It felt so perfect.

At the time, I couldn't have been happier. I was still dating Ken, and I was having sex with Dick every time he could convince his wife there was late-night work to do in the office. The dishonesty and cheating never bothered me — my search for love was finally successful and the price didn't matter.

Tom

The television shop was a busy little place with a friendly clientele. It was there that I learned to meet people and to interact without fear.

At 17, I finally felt happy and confident. Little did I know how very much farther I had to go in my search for *someone to love me*.

One afternoon, an absolutely spectacular looking guy came into the store. When I spotted him walking through the door, all that mattered to me was adding this man to my already too-full repertoire.

I completely forgot how "wonderful" my life already was with two men.

I guess it just wasn't enough for me.

With all of my practiced charm, I greeted this new challenge, "Can I help you find something, or answer any questions?"

"Well, I'm looking for a television," he replied with an appreciative smile, "but I'd like some technical advice before making a decision. I ran into the guy who owns this shop a couple of days ago, and figured he'd be able to answer my questions. Is Dick here?"

"No," I said, "I'm sorry, Dick isn't here right now. But he'll be back later this afternoon. Why don't you leave your name and a phone number where you can be reached, and I'll have Dick call as soon as he returns."

"Great," he agreed, "my name is Tom. Tell Dick to call any time." He wrote down his number and turned to leave.

My heart dropped. He couldn't leave yet! I needed more time. The only thing I could do was accompany him to the door and hope he'd stick around for a minute or two.

I walked close to him and gently touched his arm as I purred, "Thanks for stopping in. Maybe I'll see you again soon."

I was both relieved and overjoyed when Tom responded, "My pleasure for sure! By the way, are you married, or attached to anyone?"

"No," I answered with a shy grin.

"Well, then," Tom began slowly, "may I interest you in a dinner date sometime? I'd like to get to know you."

"I'd like that a lot," I said.

And I did like it.

I loved all the evenings with Tom that followed. He was so kind and considerate.

In fact, as I look back, Tom might be the only man who ever really loved me in a really unselfish way.

But, I wasn't accustomed to that kind of consideration. Under the surface, there was a nagging discomfort with Tom — maybe he was too "nice" — not enough of a fight!

Why is this so easy? Why is he so nice to me? Where *is the challenge here?*

Then, one evening my paradise with juggling three men ended. After a wonderful evening together, Tom and I were pulling into the driveway of our house and I caught my breath.

I was horrified — Ken was sitting in his car waiting for me. What a mess! All I could think of was explaining to Ken.

I didn't care what Tom was thinking or feeling. Ken was my only worry.

I jumped out of the car and ran over to Ken. Scrambling into the front seat of his car I cried, "I know how this looks, but it's not what you think. It's not important. He's just a guy that doesn't mean anything to me. Please try to understand."

Ken was furious. He pushed me away, started his car, and began to back out of the driveway.

"If you know what's good for you, you'll get out of this car right now. I never want to see you again, you lying bitch!"

I should have followed Ken's advice. But I didn't.

I cried and cried. I flung my arms around his neck and begged for just a few more minutes to explain.

"I love you," I screamed, "please don't leave me. You have to forgive me. I can't live without you."

Ken finally gave in. "OK," he said, "but get rid of that guy once and for all."

I went back to Tom, and without any remorse, demanded that he leave. I didn't care about the honest pain or the tears I saw on his face.

With a very distorted sense of reasoning, I turned my back on the man who really cared for me to salvage a relationship with a man who made me *work* for his affection. Now, as I look back, I see that choice as the first in a repeated tendency that caused a great deal of pain.

I am so sorry.

selfish love isn't love at all

Ken did at last forgive me. But it took a long time before he trusted me again. He used my "infidelity" to very subtly make me feel unworthy.

What a master Ken was at making me feel awful, but needing him at the same time!

I often wonder what Ken would have done if he'd found out about Dick! Even after Ken and I made up — and in spite of my fear of losing him — I kept sleeping with Dick during those "long work days."

But something went wrong. Almost over night, I noticed that Dick was acting less affectionate with me. And he wasn't suggesting late evenings in the office any longer.

It made me crazy. I did everything I could think of doing to get his attention. But nothing worked. He remained distant and cool to all of my nudges.

Finally, I mustered the courage, and asked, "Is there something wrong? I miss you. Are you angry at me?"

Dick looked half anxious and half relieved. "Well," he stammered, "there's really nothing wrong. I just can't see you anymore. I have someone else now."

"My wife and I are getting a divorce so I can marry her," Dick continued, "so under the circumstances, it would be better if you found another job as soon as you can."

I was stunned and angrier than I had ever been in my life.
How could he do this to me?
At the same time I was confused enough to shame him.
How could he do this to his wife and children? How could he cause so much pain
I never looked at myself closely.

foolish denial

When I was 18 years old and Ken was 29, he asked me to marry him. We had been together for almost three years.

He was my anchor. I was his toy.

We were a pretty compatible match really. Ken loved to drink and play hard, and so did I. Packing as much fun as possible into every day — that was the goal.

Ken didn't take anything or anyone very seriously. He looked at life like a party — with the attitude that things were placed on earth to give him pleasure.

I knew these things about him, but I wasn't afraid. Ken was my only ticket away from a miserable home — where my Mother and Father were still fighting.

And, most important, *he loved me.*

What I didn't know at the time was that Ken loved alcohol more than me...more than anything.

Ken and I had been married for two years when our first child was born — a perfect, tiny girl who I named Keely. Still, to this day, I remember the thrill of her.

She was so beautiful. And I loved her more than I knew was possible.

I was overwhelmed with joy. So much so it didn't seem to bother me that Ken wasn't sharing my happiness. This new little life didn't change his outlook at all.

I didn't care. She was mine — and I loved her. I didn't think about anything else.

I didn't even mind that when Ken finally arrived at the hospital for a first peek at his new baby, he was so drunk he couldn't stay awake. It didn't matter anymore. He was just being Ken.

Looking back, I realize that my new role as a Mother absorbed all my attention — and I was more than happy to give it. But in my state of blissful preoccupation, I failed to notice some real danger signs.

Ken was drunk almost all the time. He couldn't concentrate. He couldn't hold a normal conversation. He was distant and separated somehow.

I was so foolish not to see the threatening signals. We lived for years teetering on the brink of disaster — Ken, in his chemical stupor, and me, blissfully blind with my beautiful daughter.

Ken was our sole source of financial support, but he couldn't keep a job for more than a few months. He went from one job to another — always someone else's fault.

Still I didn't worry.

But three years later a new event shook me to my senses. Our second daughter was born.

Kimberly, I love you.

Looking down into that pure, wonderful face, I began to wonder, "How has this miracle come from such a hollow relationship?"

Gradually, I began to feel afraid for my children. My two daughters meant the world to me. I loved them so much.

I wanted everything in their lives to be perfect. I wanted them to have everything that I never had. Yet, I knew I was unable to supply it.

How will I take care of my precious babies without help? Ken doesn't care about us.

He couldn't. He was too sick from drinking. Ken was so out of control that the police picked him up and put him in jail, on a number of different occasions, for public drunkenness and disorderly behavior. And still he didn't stop.

Why haven't I done something to stop this downward spiral long before now? How is it that I've just ignored it?

Panic overtook my life in those first few months of Kimberly's life — and it didn't leave me for many, many years to come.

I spent many nights crying myself to sleep, alone and scared. It felt the same as when I was a little girl so desperately searching for *someone to love me.*

empty promises

When Keely was five, Ken was offered a new job with a company located in Grand Rapids, a city about 75 miles from our house in Lansing. At first, I was hopeful. I kept thinking that a new job might be just the boost Ken needed to make a change.

Oh yes, things changed. But not for the better. Our lives began a slow, but sure descent.

Ken was so dependent on alcohol, he started drinking as soon as he was done working.

Sometimes, if he could manage, he drove back to our house in Lansing. But that was unusual. Most of the time, he didn't come home at all.

Ken had other women. I knew it, but I chose not to think about it. I didn't know what to do.

I just wanted us to be a family. I tried to look pretty...I kept the house nice and clean...I took good care of our children...and I begged for his attention.

Finally, when our Keely was ready to begin first grade, and Kimberly was three, Ken agreed to move to Grand Rapids. And again, I dared to hope.

We were able to buy a cute little house in East Grand Rapids. And, for a while, I was so excited about our new surroundings, I forgot to worry about the seriousness of my problems.

Keely started at her new school and loved it. Everything seemed better. I worked in the house and played with my girls. I felt happier than I had been in a long time. Maybe I would have a *real* family after all.

But the cuffs of alcoholism are very tight. They don't let go.

Ken couldn't stop drinking. In spite of my dreams, I found myself raising my daughters in the same kind of home I had so desperately wanted to escape.

please, Daddy

By the time Keely and Kim were both in school, they understood (as well as little children can) that their Father was emotionally absent — but they didn't understand why. Even when Ken was home, he lived in a world of his own — and it was a world that didn't include us.

The girls sat by the window and waited for their daddy to come home after work. But he always arrived with the same darkened mood...staggered walk...blank face...and slurred speech.

If Ken talked to us at all, it was usually in anger. More often than not, he would just go somewhere else in the house to avoid having to deal with us.

For some reason, my daughters, just like I had done years before, refused to give up. They wanted their daddy so badly. They wanted his attention.

They begged for his affection.

But they never knew his love.

Keely and Kim teased and teased until Ken agreed to be at birthday parties and special school programs. I can still see their little eyes looking at him when they asked, "Please, Daddy, will you come? Can you be there with us?"

Time after time, Ken promised. "Okay, okay," he muttered, "just drop it."

But, in spite of his promises, he only showed up once.

It was the time Keely had a singing part in the school Christmas program.

The night before, she put her arms around his legs and looked up at her Father with her final plea. "Will you come home for the program right after work — before you go out drinking?" she asked.

Ken promised. But he came late. And he came drunk. I will never forget the disappointment in my daughter's face.

As I look back at that night, I think it triggered changes to come. The experience forced me into giving up my dreams and into admitting the truth about my husband and his effects on our family.

I faced the fact that Ken was showing the signs of advanced alcoholism. He was gone almost every night until two or three o'clock in the morning. He couldn't walk. He couldn't talk. Sometimes he was sick with the stench of vomit all over himself.

I had to finally admit we meant absolutely nothing to Ken. Although he shared our address, and was legally a husband and father, he abandoned his family just as surely as if he had left us altogether.

I didn't know what to do. My two daughters were everything to me. I loved them and so very much wanted the best for them. I really did try to be everything to both of them. I gave them all the love a Mother could give to her children.

But I could not give them the love of their Father.

I was very lonely...frightened...worried.

Kevin

One afternoon my girlfriend called to ask if I could go out for dinner. Her husband was going to be working late, and she thought it would be fun for "us women" to go out for a nice evening away from home.

Well, that sounded like a dream vacation to me. So I did the unthinkable. I agreed to go even though I knew Ken would strangle me if he ever found out. I found a baby sitter for the girls and off I went.

We went to a very nice restaurant and settled in with a before-dinner cocktail and girl talk. Oh, it felt wonderful to be away from the worries of home even for a few hours.

I didn't plan for what happened that night. But I certainly didn't protest either.

After dinner, we moved into the lounge for "one more drink." A dance band was playing soft music and it was a pleasant, comfortable place.

People were happy and having a good time. I felt as though I'd taken a leap into paradise.

Before I noticed him approaching, a man was standing at our table looking at me with an inviting smile. I looked up and in one moment developed a severe case of selective memory.

Suddenly I was a single woman again, desperately looking for *someone to love me.*

All I could think about was that this had to be the best-looking man I'd ever seen. We smiled a greeting at each other, and he said, "Hi, my name is Kevin, and I'm wondering if my friend and I may join you two?"

I tossed a glance at my girlfriend and was given a mischievous nod.

With her silent approval, I looked back at Kevin and shyly agreed. "Sure," I responded, "that would be nice."

From that time on, nothing existed in the room but Kevin and me. He was funny, kind, intelligent, and so, so appealing.

Kevin's attention gave me new hope...new motives. Suddenly life didn't seem so desolate any longer.

I had a wonderful time that night. I didn't want the fantasy to be over. I remember wishing that time would stand still.

But it didn't. I started watching the clock and becoming more and more nervous about the girls at home with the sitter — and even more worried that Ken would appear at home earlier than usual and catch me away.

Kevin noticed my discomfort. "We'd better call it a night," he said, "but would it be okay for me to call you next week? Maybe we could meet for lunch."

Kevin looked straight into my eyes, and softly put his arms around me.

"Oh, please do," I whispered.

Kevin kissed me goodnight. And I left for home fully expecting that my life would never be the same.

In a way, my life did change.

But in a much greater way, it stayed the same.

Over the next few days I was on pins and needles waiting for Kevin to call. I couldn't think about anything else. I wanted so much to be loved again.

Finally, one afternoon, the phone rang and answering it I heard Kevin's voice, "Hi, Kevin, here. How are you?"

"Hello, Kevin. I'm just great! How about you?" I answered trying to sound nonchalant.

"Well, I'm fine, but I'd be a lot better if you'd agree to meet for lunch tomorrow?" Kevin teased.

And I was more than ready to agree.

I was ecstatic.

My dreams are about to come true...every thing's going to be okay now.

After that first lunch, I was hooked. I needed him in my life to help me forget the sorry mess it was in.

The sheer anticipation of a new love all but shrouded the misery threatening my home and family. In the excitement of those first few encounters, I failed to notice that I was headed for repeating the mistake I'd made before.

I was working from a place of emotional need rather than common sense.

I didn't care that Kevin was married. So was I, after all. He was unhappy too. And of course, all the problems with his wife were out of his control — not his fault or doing.

I was such a fool. I was ready to cooperate in any way Kevin suggested to just to see him now and then.

I was content with scraps of affection. I needed *someone to love me* so badly... and kiss me good night...and hold me...and tell me I was his special girl.

I was obsessed with finding someone to say all the words my Father never said to me.

I searched for love from Kevin for two years. But I didn't find the real thing.

truth or consequences

At home Ken was drinking more and more — and beginning to lose total control. He was becoming a regular resident in the city jail after being picked up by police for public disruptions or drunk driving.

As for me, I was starting to show the signs of stress too. Living two lives — both full of dishonesty and co-dependent behavior — is bound to take its toll. I was frightened. I was nervous. I was tired.

I was shedding weight fast and I was losing my ability to function like a normal person. I couldn't drive the car, or go into crowds of people.

I couldn't stop the symptoms and I was becoming worried that my children would notice. So, as a last resort, I made an appointment with a doctor, who after a brief consultation, offered the perfect solution.

Valium!

The drug was a miracle. Each little pill made the fear and tension go away. I felt like a new woman.

Over time, with my valium boosters, I grew stronger and less afraid. And with my new-found confidence I resolved one more time to make my marriage work.

I devised a plan to be the best wife a woman could be. I thought maybe if I succeeded, Ken would love me and the girls again, and we could be a real family.

So, I waited on Ken hand and foot. I made certain to look beautiful when he came home every night. I promised never to complain. I disciplined the children when their playfulness irked their Father. But none of these efforts changed anything.

Then I came up with another idea — a new baby!

32

Surely, if Ken knows he has another child, he'll snap to his senses and come back to us.

So, without telling Ken of my plan, I tried to get pregnant. And after a few months of strategically timed efforts, I was expecting another baby.

I was so happy knowing that there was a new little life growing in me. Better yet, so was Ken! At last it seemed that everything was going to be just fine.

It's a blessing we can't see into the future, because I couldn't have been more wrong.

During the fifth month, my water broke and I was rushed to the hospital. After a complete examination, the doctor said that if I wanted to save my baby I would have to stay in bed for the rest of my pregnancy.

I wanted my baby to live, so I did everything I was told. I laid in bed all day and all night. I prayed and prayed — hoping that there was a god listening who would take care of my baby.

But something was very wrong. After almost two weeks, I was rushed back to the hospital with the beginning of labor pains.

I was so panicky. I knew it was too early for my baby. I tried to will them away, but I couldn't stop the pains.

Three days of hard labor followed. At the end of that third horrible day, my little Carrie was born.

And after a few brief seconds of life, my little Carrie died.

I remember the reaction of the nurse in the delivery room. At first sight of Carrie, the nurse caught her breath and quietly cried, "Oh, no!"

I knew from watching her face when she saw my baby that something was very wrong. I begged to hold my precious newborn, but they wouldn't let me even see her.

They rushed me from delivery to a recovery room, where I waited and waited for what felt like an eternity.

Finally, a male nurse came into the room, walked up to my bed, and with a stern, unemotional voice he said, "Your baby is dead."

Over and over I cried out, "Why? Why my baby?"

I cried for hours and hours all alone. I cannot describe the pain. There are no words to define the feelings of loss.

When Ken finally arrived at the hospital, he was so drunk he didn't even realize what was happening. When I saw him, I hated him. At last I knew that he would never really love me.

I was never allowed to see my third daughter. But, I will never forget her as long as I live.

I know that someday, when I get to heaven, I will finally hold my baby girl.

Thank you, Jesus, for taking care of my little angel.

Resolve

Pain teaches lessons. Losing something very, very precious to us often helps point out what's really important.

When I came home from the hospital, the only thing I wanted to do was hold Keely and Kim, and tell them how much I loved them.

But even though I wanted to, I couldn't shut myself in with my girls forever. So I focused on getting through one day at a time.

Slowly but surely I managed to get our life back to normal — at least normal for us.

And sure enough, it wasn't long before everything was the same. Ken was drinking. He was blatantly seeing other women. He was mean and angry.

I was so unhappy...so lonely...so afraid. I existed on valium.

One thing *was* different, however. I finally admitted that there was absolutely nothing I could do to make Ken love me. I knew he would never be able or willing to take care of us no matter how hard I tried to gain his affection.

Gradually, I gave up looking to Ken for support and decided to take matters into my own hands. The children were older and they needed things we simply couldn't afford with the money Ken had left over after his nightly binges.

I went looking for a job and found a receptionist opening in an attorney's office. I knew right away that it was going to be a stretch for me, but I also knew there wasn't any other option — life couldn't go on the way it was. The girls needed me to do this.

I realized not long after starting work at the law office that, if I wanted to keep the job, I'd better settle down and focus. The attorneys were busy and the tasks assigned to me were more detailed than any responsibilities I'd ever been given before.

It made me nervous. I really wanted to do something *right* for a change.

I could deal with the work stress by taking valium all day long. It made me feel level-headed and capable. At the time, I wasn't even aware of how dependent I had become.

But dependent I was. I remember the panic that set in when I ran out of pills during the day, or when I noticed my prescription had expired. Without admitting it, I knew that without my valium pills, I simply couldn't get through the day in one piece.

Then for night-time relief I discovered another help mate. It was alcohol.

When the girls were in bed, I fixed myself a couple of drinks. A bit of vodka on top off those daily valium doses made the long nights alone seem not so bad at all.

It is still amazing to me how quickly chemical dependencies can take control of our lives if we let them. And even more amazing are the long-lasting effects chemical dependencies have on our lives and on those we love.

One evening, when I came home from work, the girls met me at the door. I realized instantly that something was very wrong from the wary expressions on their faces.

I don't remember why, but Ken stayed home from work that day. And he must have been drinking for a long time, because by the time I got home he was laying on the couch in a drunk stupor.

Apparently, when Keely and Kim came home from school, they interrupted his binge. The girl's weren't used to Ken being home — especially in the afternoon. They didn't understand that they were expected to leave him alone.

Ken was angry and hateful. "Can't a guy have a little peace and quiet in his own house once in a while?" he screamed.

Keely ran over to him, put her hands on her hips, and shouted, "Don't yell at us. You're the one who's drunk, Daddy! We haven't done anything wrong."

Before I could get to Keely, Ken reached out and swung. His fist slammed across her little face. I caught her as she reeled back.

I was horrified. I pushed Keely behind me and shouted at Ken to stop. But he was out of control.

In a flash, the sleeping giant turned into a monster. Ken's whole appearance changed in a single instant.

He looked like a totally different person. His face...his eyes...even his body posture...his whole being seemed to project a violence so dangerous it scared us all to death.

I grabbed the girls and ran into the kitchen.

Get away from him...get the girls far away.

Something snapped in his head. Ken didn't care whom he hurt or how much. And I was his next victim.

Ken came after me with such speed and strength, I couldn't react in time. He hit me so hard I flew backward off the floor and slammed into the kitchen door.

Keely and Kim ran to me. They were both crying, "Mommy, mommy!" Their eyes glared with terror and wonder.

Suddenly, I realized their young innocence was gone forever. I was so frightened for them...and for myself.

Fortunately, I didn't hit my head hard enough to knock me out of my senses. I struggled to my feet. I tucked Keely and Kim between me and the door. And I braced myself for another impact.

But when I looked up, Ken was gone! It was over— at least for now.

At that moment, I vowed that nothing like this would ever happen again. I resolved to make a change. I knew I had to get my daughters and myself far away from Ken.

The torture and torment were going to stop.

The very next day, I filed for divorce. Several days later, Ken was served the papers. When he finally figured out he didn't have any other options, he moved out of the house.

I was so happy to see him go.

At 35 years old, I was facing the prospect of being truly self-dependent for the first time in my life.

And the truth is — Connie, Keely, and Kimberly managed to pick up the pieces of our lives better than I could ever have imagined. We got along surprisingly well!

I continued working at the law office. The girls slowly recuperated from their fear. And everything felt more settled and comfortable than our home had ever been.

But it wasn't long before the instinct to find *someone to love me* reared its ugly head again. It was a stubborn need.

Jerry

One afternoon — several months before my divorce from Ken was final — I was working on daily time reports when a familiar face entered the office. It was Jerry. He was an insurance underwriter and a regular visitor with the attorneys.

I smiled a friendly greeting and asked, "Who's expecting you, Jerry? I'll let them know you're here."

"Well, actually," Jerry responded with a sly smile, "I don't have an appointment. I just stopped in to see if *you're* free for lunch tomorrow."

My head reeled.

Another chance at love! I know it will be different this time.

"Oh, my gosh, I wasn't expecting this!" I replied quietly, "but, thank you, Jerry, I'd like that very much."

"Great!" Jerry replied sincerely, "I'll come by for you just before noon tomorrow. See you then, Connie."

I went home so happy. I couldn't wait until the next day. It was fun to think about looking pretty for someone who cared again...it was fun to plan my offense.

That first lunch date was just the beginning of a phase in my life that still haunts me.

Jerry turned out to be much, much more than just male attention. He was 53 years old, mature, wise, affectionate, and caring.

He was the father figure I'd never had.

We saw a lot of each other. I thought he was the greatest. He made me feel so safe.

But, Keely and Kim didn't agree. They didn't like the new romance at all. And nothing I said changed their mind.

I'm not sure whether they disliked *Jerry*... disliked *seeing me* with Jerry...or whether their trepidation was the result of an overall fear of *men in general,* but Keely and Kim hated everything about him.

I didn't know at the time that they were more intuitive than I was. Now I know that I should have heeded my daughters' protests.

But instead of holding Jerry at arm's length, I made Jerry my life. Not a moment passed when I wasn't trying to please him. I loved being with him. And I believed every promise he made *to take care of us forever.*

Then the bottom fell out of my life. I found out I was pregnant again!

What should have been such a joyful time in my life turned into a nightmare. There I was going through a divorce while expecting a new baby by another man. I was taunted by my own fears.

What will people say? I can't let anyone know. What will Jerry say? What should I do?

When I told Jerry that I was pregnant, my worst fears became reality. He was so angry. He blamed me as though I had created this problem alone, and on purpose.

He kept saying, "Connie, I've got five grandchildren. The last thing I need is another child. What in the hell are you thinking?"

I didn't know what to do. I laid at night scared of what people would think — my bosses...my daughters... Ken...my lawyer...the judge.

God, what a mess. By the time I get to court for my divorce, I'll look pregnant. Everyone will know for sure.

I pleaded with Jerry for understanding and looked to him for advice. But he didn't seem to feel as though it was his problem at all. It was mine alone.

Jerry's only suggestion was to eliminate the problem altogether. He said, "Oh, Connie, don't make such a big deal out of this. Just get an abortion. It's the only way out of this."

I didn't want an abortion — not because I thought it was the wrong thing to do at the time — but because I loved the thought of having another child.

But I was scared of losing Jerry if I refused.

He was really adamant about the awful consequences of keeping my baby. "I don't want another child," he said, "just remember, if you go through with this, you'll be doing it alone! I don't have the time or money for another kid."

Fearing the loss of Jerry's love, I listened to him instead of my own heart. And as long as I live I will always regret that choice.

My baby could have lived...laughed...and loved. But I chose to end that tiny life.

I went to the clinic alone. It was cold. It was quiet. It was frightening. I don't think I ever felt so alone.

There's a life inside me. I'm really not alone here. But, baby, I'm not giving you a chance or a choice.

I was heart broken.

I went home by myself and fell in bed. I felt so empty, depressed, and tired. But I kept rationalizing my choices.

Well, it's over now. A t least I don't have to worry anymore. Jerry will be pleased. I can get on with my life and Jerry will love me.

But now I know that abortions only end the lives of babies. They don't solve problems. They don't insure that relationships will last. And they don't eliminate the memories.

Today, there's not a day that passes that I don't think of you *Baby.* I wonder who you were. I wonder what you would look like. My heart breaks for each lost day.

I *love you my little one.*

a useless sacrifice

Three months later my divorce was final. Ken was gone, and I was so relieved. I knew in my heart that my problems were over.

I called Jerry to make celebration plans and got quite a shock. "Hi, honey," I greeted enthusiastically, "It's over. I'm free. Let's go out and celebrate tonight. Can we?"

"Sorry, Connie. I've already made other plans with someone else," Jerry answered and stopped short.

I caught my breath. The silence lasted forever.

Could I be hearing this right? Jerry with someone else? No! It can't be! He promised to love me!

39

"What do you mean?" I whispered.

"I *mean* I'm seeing someone else, Connie. That's all," Jerry said matter-of-factly.

I was heartbroken and full of panic. I needed him so much. I couldn't believe Jerry would do this tome.

What was I going to do? Who would I find to take care of me?

I had never even considered that it was possible to live without a man in my life!

Things were pretty rough for a while. I was forced to sell the house as a condition of my divorce agreement. We moved into an apartment across town. The girls had to leave their school, neighborhood, and friends. They were so unhappy...lonely...disoriented.

And so was I.

Jerry was gone with his new woman. I had *no one to love me.*

My nerves were pushed to the limit by fear, depression, and my vain attempts stay calm through an abusive use of valium. Depression and panic got so bad that on some days I couldn't even leave the apartment. I got the girls off to school and went back to bed.

I found myself calling work and reporting in *sick* way too often. I began to worry that someone would notice and I'd lose my job.

I called Jerry and begged him to come back, but he just hung up the phone when he heard my voice. I needed help badly. I was scared.

I remember thinking — *I can't do this alone.*

I was losing my ability to live a normal life. But what worried me most was the threat of not being able to take care of my girls. It got to a point that I knew I had to get professional help.

I found a psychiatrist and took his first open appointment time. The thought of talking to a complete stranger made me a little nervous, but then I didn't have a choice.

Nervous... what else is new? I'll just take an extra dose of valium and it'll be okay!

Before I left the apartment that day I did take my valium, but it didn't work as well as I hoped. By the time I got to the doctor's office, I was pushing back a panic attack with all my might.

It took every ounce of energy I could muster to explain that all my problems were somehow related to Jerry.

If he would only come back, everything would be fine again. I needed him.

Of course, my doctor told me my problems were much deeper and more serious than just losing a relationship with Jerry.

"Connie," he explained, "you can't go through life *needing* love from another person just to function! You can't always control how another person feels about you. But you *can* control how you feel about yourself. Lets work on that shall we?"

When I left that first appointment, I really started to think about what I'd been told. And it made sense!

In fact, it was the first time in my life that I stopped to analyze my feelings and why I acted the way I did. I really wanted to be stronger...to feel less afraid...and to find happiness *without* depending on *someone to love me.*

When I returned to the apartment that afternoon, I felt a lot better. I was determined to make a difference for myself...for Keely...for Kim.

It's strange the way things work out. That same afternoon, I received a telephone call from a friend who lived in our old neighborhood. She knew I hated moving the girls across town, and she phoned to tell me there was a house for rent right across the street from our old home.

It was a great home for us! The girls could go back to their school and friends. It was such a pretty little house too.

I called the owner to ask about the rent amount and was overjoyed when they told me it was only a few dollars a month more than the apartment.

"Great! I can afford that," I blurted out, "it's perfect for us. Can we have it? I'll come right over and sign the lease if you agree!"

I think he sensed and appreciated my enthusiasm, because he laughed and said as soon as we could take care of the paperwork, the house was ours.

What excitement! The girls and I were literally jumping with joy.

We packed up and moved to our new home in a matter of weeks. We were so happy the first few months.

I was faithful in going for therapy. And it was helping. I was learning to understand myself and understand why I felt so afraid. There were fewer panic attacks and my need to take valium diminished substantially. I felt stronger and more independent than I had ever before.

But only after a few happy months on our own, Jerry showed up again. I answered the phone one night and practically fainted when I heard his voice.

Jerry was practically crying when he said, "Connie, I'm so sorry. I'm such a fool. I made a horrible mistake. I love *you*. Will you forgive me?"

I was so surprised. I hadn't figured on hearing from Jerry ever again, and what's more, I was trying very hard not to care!

But without thinking, I answered, "Oh, Jerry. I love you too!"

He came right over to the house. And our relationship rekindled as though there had never been a break.

We spent a lot of time together. There were trips to Las Vegas... dozens of roses...wonderful nights of dinners and dancing...and many comfortable evenings at home.

But all was not perfect. I began to notice that Jerry had a serious health problem.

When I pressured him for answers, Jerry explained that he was taking pills for a heart condition, but he assured me it wasn't serious.

Jerry didn't look well, however. He acted tired and his face was beginning to show the strain. He had intermittent spells where he couldn't even walk across the room.

Gradually Jerry became weaker and weaker. And in the process, I saw less and less of him.

There really wasn't one day that we decided not to see each other anymore. Our times together just became less regular and the phone calls farther and farther apart — until all contact practically ceased to exist.

Bill

Keely was now in her first year at high school, and Kim was in sixth grade. We were happy together and supportive of each other.

I think if I had stopped to examine that time in my life, I would have been really surprised to discover I was actually satisfied without a man in my life. I had become content with loving my children. It was enough.

But I didn't stop to examine my situation. I wasn't looking for *someone to love me* with such urgency anymore, but the new me wasn't the result of a conscious choice. It had just happened.

If I *had* been wise enough to make better choices, maybe the horror of the next few years never would have happened.

One warm, autumn evening, the girls and I were together in the back yard, cooking dinner on the grill. Suddenly, I noticed a man walking up the driveway toward us.

At first, I felt alarmed, but when I studied him closer, I knew we'd met before. He was a handsome man and his face was familiar, but I couldn't remember who he was.

He smiled at us and waved a greeting. "Hey, Connie. Bill Sharp is the name," he hollered, "nice to see you again!"

Then I remembered him. Bill and his wife lived next door to our old house before Ken and I were divorced.

"Hi, Bill. It's nice to see you too! What are you doing here?" I asked.

"Oh, I had some free time this afternoon, so I thought I'd drive through the old neighborhood and reminisce a bit," Bill answered a little sadly.

"My wife and I broke up too, and it's been a pretty rough year."

I felt a pang of sympathy for him. I remembered how lonely it made me feel to go through a divorce. And besides, he looked like such a nice, sensitive guy.

Gosh, it's too bad these things happen to such nice people. That woman must be a fool!

"Well, I'm glad you came back to say 'Hello'," I said. "You're just in time for a burger if you don't mind eating with the mosquitoes in the back yard!"

"Hey, yeah," Bill responded with genuine surprise. "I sure didn't come looking for an invitation, but I'm not going to turn it down either."

We had a good time talking about everything under the sun. We confided in each other about our marriages, jobs, children, disappointments, and dreams. It felt so good to have somebody to talk to...who listened with real interest...and who felt some of the same hurts and fears I experienced.

I discovered that Bill worked in "capital investment sales." And apparently he was quite successful. (Of course, I didn't have the slightest idea what he meant by "capital investments," so anything he told me would have been just fine!)

Bill was only a few years older than me. And he had the best personality — so bright and easy to talk to. He made me laugh. We had fun that afternoon. And so did the girls.

I was sad to see our spontaneous picnic with our new friend end. It was the first time in a long while that the girls and I had enjoyed visiting with a guest.

"I'd better get going," Bill said looking at his watch, "it's getting late, and I don't want to wear out my welcome. But, would it be okay if I called to see you again some time?"

"Of course," I laughed, "I'd like that and so would Keely and Kim."

I didn't know it then, but with that agreement, I was about to enter another chapter in my life that would change it forever.

Bill and I began dating regularly, and then moved into a very committed relationship. We had a wonderful time together. I simply didn't think I could ask for anyone better.

Bill made me feel as though I was the most beautiful woman in the world. He sent me flowers every week...took me to the finest places...and showered me with beautiful clothes and jewelry.

I figured he must have been very successful in his career to have so much extra money. But Bill never talked about work. He just always had an ample amount to spend.

Best of all, Bill was so attentive. He was always checking on me. He didn't let a day go by without calling to make sure I was okay... where I was going...what I was doing...who I was with.

He loved me so much.

And everyone in my life approved. Keely and Kim liked Bill almost as much as I did. My family and friends adored him too.

"What a catch," they'd say, "you're so lucky, Connie!"

I knew without a doubt that I had found *someone to love me,* and that he who would love me forever.

I finally had a man to hold me...kiss me goodnight...kiss me good morning...and tell me I was his special girl.

In December 1974, I found out I was pregnant. So Bill and I were married in January 1975.

We were so happy standing together in church that morning. Keely and Kim were there with us. Everything seemed perfect.

Even now, as I recall my wedding day, my eyes sting with tears. That wonderful feeling was so very short-lived.

Nothing was as it seemed. I was headed for more torment than I could have ever thought possible.

Trapped

Love Shouldn't be so Painful

Domestic violence and abuse is a national crisis. There are far too many women who could paint, from experience, a very realistic picture of hell on earth. They live every minute of every day in dread and fear of the person who "loves" them.

They wonder what nasty, belittling words he'll scream: "You fat, ugly bitch. You can't do anything right. Don't you have a brain in your head? Who taught you to keep house....look at this dump. You're damn lucky I come home at all!"

They hope with every ounce of their being he won't get so angry that he'll hit them again — or something worse. It's true — he threatens more than anything, but it's still so frightening. "Watch out, or I'll slap the s--- out of you. And if you don't shut up those kids, I'll teach them a lesson too." They really never know what will happen or when. How do they trigger such anger?

It's a horrible way to live — but the alternative seems even worse. Victims caught in abusive relationships worry: "What if he leaves me? There is nowhere else to go. No one else would love me." And this is the essence of the hell — there is no hope.

When all the shouting is done, when the threat is gone, when it's finally quiet and there is a safe place to be alone and think for a while — then maybe some answers will come: "What did I do? There must be a better way. I've got to get out of here!"

It's never too soon— or too late.

After our marriage, Bill and I and the girls lived in our little rental house. For a few weeks, I was happier than I had ever been in my life. All four of us were in love with each other, and we were all looking forward to our new baby on the way.

Then the bottom fell out.

Three months to the day after Bill and I were married, on a rainy Saturday afternoon, the doorbell rang. We were surprised — knowing we weren't expecting anyone, and wondering who would be out on such a miserable day.

When I opened the door, I was more than surprised to see two police officers staring back at me.

"Mrs. Sharp?" one officer asked.

"Yes?" I answered with the same questioning tone.

"We need to speak with your husband," he responded, "is Bill home with you?"

"Yes. He's here — in the living room with my daughters. But what do you want with him?" I asked, pulling the door open as an invitation for the officers to come in the house.

"We need to speak with Bill first, Ma'am. Our business is with him," an officer answered, "but we'll fill you in before we leave."

When I turned to find Bill, he was already walking toward me and our two unexpected guests. When I saw the look on his face, I knew immediately that something was terribly wrong. His eyes darted from me to the officers with an expression of resignation and genuine sadness.

Bill was arrested for embezzlement and was gone within thirty minutes. He stood so quietly looking at the floor as one police officer read his rights and the other put handcuffs around his wrist.

The officer looked at me and explained, "I'm sorry, Mrs. Sharp. We have to take him to jail for these charges. He should stand trial in a few weeks, but he'll have to stay behind bars until then. Here's the phone number you can call for more information."

I took the slip of paper offered me and stood frozen in place. I was paralyzed...unable to talk...unable to move as I watched my husband being escorted to the police cruiser. I wanted to run to Bill, but he never looked back at me.

Four weeks later I sat behind Bill in a cold, sparsely populated courtroom. We both sat motionlessly as the sentence was passed.

I will remember forever the hollow, echoing sound of the judge's voice as he pronounced the words, "Three to five years in the state penitentiary."

I was stunned.

Three to five years. What would I do? I was pregnant.

How could I explain this to Keely and Kim? They had just learned to trust a man again...and they loved their stepfather.

I left the court room in shock. I don't remember walking back to the parking lot, or even driving home. There were only fear... questions... despair...and a constant flow of tears streaming down my face.

The man I married embezzled over one million dollars from people who thought they were investing money in a mobile home park! I just couldn't believe it.

When I got home, I told the girls what had happened. They were speechless and almost as scared as I was.

We hadn't kept secrets from each other. They knew I didn't have any income of my own — or even savings stashed away for an emergency.

Together, my daughters and I faced the harsh truth. We were dependent on Bill, and realized the danger too late.

After I settled down a little, I phoned Bill's brother and his mother for two reasons. First, I knew I had to let them know what happened. But I also wanted to see if either one would offer to help us out for a while — at least until I could find another job.

My brother- and mother-in-law were both pretty well set financially. But after talking with each, it became very apparent that neither was interested in even hearing about our problems, much less helping us out with them. They simply couldn't care less what happened to Bill or his new family.

I felt so alone...so ashamed. I went to great lengths to cover up Bill's whereabouts. I told everyone Bill was out of the country on an extended business trip.

I tried to find a job, and couldn't. Nobody wanted to hire a desperate, pregnant woman with two underage children and no husband at home.

The panic attacks returned. The fear was unbearable.

How am I going to support my daughters and my unborn baby? How could this happen to me again?

Finally, I went to the Social Services Department and applied for welfare support. And about one month later we began receiving a monthly check from the state along with food stamps.

At least we had enough money for the rent and groceries. But I can remember feeling so embarrassed...so diminished.

I went grocery shopping late at night or early in the morning when no one else was there — nobody I knew at least. Then I stalked around until I found a checkout lane with no people waiting in line so no one would see me using food stamps.

Bill used his prison phone privileges regularly to call home. But, I guess he called for a change of pace, and simply because he didn't have anyone else to contact.

He expressed little remorse for his mistakes and how it was affecting us. Nor did he ever show a bit of concern for what was happening. I kept waiting for him to apologize...to ask how we were doing...and to offer some helpful suggestions. But he never did.

Bill's selfishness should have been a warning. But in spite of my disappointment, I chose not to heed the caution signals.

I drove to Jackson Prison every week. The facility was huge, cold, and ugly. The guards had to search me every visit, and afterward I usually had to wait for two hours or more before Bill was brought into the visiting unit. The waiting was terrible — so many silent, resigned faces staring at each other.

At first, I hated going. It was a nasty, unfriendly place. But I figured it was my duty. I loved Bill, and wanted him to know it.

Eventually, I got used to the visits — except one thing. I hated watching Bill get thinner and thinner. Over time he seemed to be slipping away from me.

He became so depressed and isolated. I felt so sorry for him. But there wasn't anything I could do to help.

By the time I was six months pregnant, I was a nervous wreck — no income...two daughters depending on me...another child on the way...and a husband in prison. I couldn't find anything to look forward to. There didn't seem to be any bright spots in my future.

I returned to my old coping habits — at least two valium and a pack of cigarettes every day, plus a few drinks before bed. It got *me* through.

But it took its toll on my *unborn baby.*

When I was exactly seven months into my pregnancy, I woke up in the middle of the night in undeniable pain. I knew in an instant what it was. I was in labor.

I remember the panic. I couldn't catch my breath. My head was pounding. The black silence seemed to close in around me. I sat up and pleaded in the darkness.

Oh, no! Not again. I love you, Baby. Stop, it's too soon!

The pains wouldn't stop, and I knew I had to get to the hospital. I dressed as quickly as I could. I woke Keely and Kim. And off we went, full of both fear and anticipation.

When I got to the hospital, I told the emergency nurse what was happening. She acted quickly, but in the rush I saw her pause and look around for a husband.

When she glanced back at me with a questioning expression on her face, I said, "The baby's Father is in Europe, but I've left a message for him. He'll be calling soon."

Appeased, the nurse engaged all the right emergency support. The delivery room was readied...physicians were on hand...and pediatricians were standing by.

In less than an hour, my little Christopher was born almost two-and-a-half months early. He only weighed three pounds. He was so tiny. But, he was so beautiful.

I held him close to me and repeated over and over again, "I love you, Christopher. I won't let you die. You'll be okay, sweetheart. Be strong."

Christopher *was* strong. He made it.

After three weeks of intensive neonatal care, my little Christopher was allowed to come home from the hospital.

What a celebration! The girls and I were thrilled. Keely and Kim cuddled and kissed their new baby brother from the moment he awoke until he fell asleep again.

It was so much fun taking care of a baby again. And, oh how Christopher responded to our loving. He giggled and smiled. He was a wonderful baby.

But although I was happy and relieved to have a healthy son, I still felt uneasy, depressed, and lonely. I sensed that something was missing in my life.

My Mother was busy working on her third marriage, but she and my new stepfather were never too busy to call and send us money whenever they could. She was my strength for a long time. And it was because of her support that we grew closer than we had ever been.

Bill's family never did call.

And even Bill didn't seem too interested. When I expressed my sadness to him over the phone (which I really tried *not* to do), he always said the same thing, "Oh, for Pete's sake, Connie, buck up. I'll be home soon and everything will be okay."

There was a huge, empty hole that no amount of valium, cigarettes, or vodka could fill. But, believe me, I kept trying.

I increased my daily allowances of each. By the time baby Chris was only one month old, my dependencies on all three habits had become serious addictions. I was trapped and didn't know it.

home again

On Christmas Eve, 1976 — nine months after Bill was sentenced to prison — there was knock at the front door. When I opened it, I couldn't believe my eyes. Bill was standing there on the porch holding a shopping bag and looking back at me with a silly grin on his face.

"Hi, Honey!" he said quietly. "I'm back. It's all over!"

He was home. What a Christmas present!

We were all so happy to see him. Now everything was going to be all right. If only I could have seen into the future.

It didn't take long to realize that the Bill living with us now was not the same man I married. It seemed as though he'd lost his heart and soul. He'd lost his passion for life altogether.

Bill refused to integrate back into our family life. He paid no attention to the girls. He wouldn't even hold his new son.

Bill displayed a completely different personality. He rarely had a kind word for any of us.

And he was so irritable. Simple things like our dog barking sent him into fits of rage — first he hit the dog and then he turned his fists on me.

When it was all over he acted as if nothing had happened. No explanations. No apologies.

Part of the problem may have been that, with his record, Bill had a hard time convincing anyone to hire him. We continued to live on my welfare income. But it was far from an easy life.

Bill finally found a job selling cars. It wasn't assured or steady income, but at least it helped salvage his broken pride. Slowly but surely, he seemed to feel a little better about himself.

the *heartbreak and guilt*

By the time Christopher was eleven months old, a quiet, but steady alarm kept ringing in my ears.

Something is wrong with my son.

The signs had become too evident and consistent. I couldn't ignore them any longer. He wasn't developing the motor and cognitive skills that normal one-year-olds should have.

Little Christopher was sick way too much. I was in and out of the hospital with him all the time.

He had respiratory problems that were so serious I had to rush him to the hospital for emergency treatments. Chris and I spent many nights in the hospital — he enclosed in an oxygen tent and me dozing nearby.

And to make matters worse, the poor little tyke had one ear infection after another. I felt so sorry for him.

Chris was so determined to be good. He tried to be quiet. But his ears hurt so badly, he couldn't help it — he just cried and cried.

Then, when Chris was about 18 months old, I was horrified to notice that his left eye wasn't focusing properly. It started to "rove" inward.

After a series of tests, the doctor informed me that Chris was practically blind in that eye. He also explained that while there was a treatment that could help cosmetically, Chris's vision loss was irreparable.

During his first three years, I did everything I could do for Chris. I found the best specialists to advise about his problems. I found money for the best treatments. I encouraged my little trooper with every bit of love I could muster to keep trying. And he did.

In spite of all his struggles, little Christopher was a very happy child. He did his best to smile through each challenge.

Then, when he was three years old, Chris and I had to face our ultimate challenge — the reality we would live with for the rest of our lives. It was determined by child development specialists that Chris had learning disabilities. He would always be in need of special education programs, and he would always face the stigma of being "abnormal."

I was so scared for him.

How would he make it through this rotten, hard life?

It was as if someone slapped me in the face. I looked at myself and had no choice but to admit that I'd made a mess out of my life, and now the rubble had passed on to poor little Chris.

I had made such irresponsible choices — the worst of which was thinking only of myself and my own fears the whole time I was pregnant. I knew better, but I continued to smoke and swallow valium and vodka every day I was pregnant.

Now Chris had to pay the consequences. What a loser I am!

It was all my fault! Chris would have a difficult life because of my selfish mistakes.

warning signs

Bill didn't seem to care one way or another about Chris — or anyone else for that matter. He managed to detach himself from each of us and everything going on in our home.

It was almost as though Bill wasn't there at all...except when he got angry. And when he was angry, we paid attention!

Most of the time, we didn't have any warning. Anything could set him off.

Keely and Kim were Bill's favorite targets. He chased them around the house, screaming at the top of his lungs.

Another of Bill's favorite scare tactics was to stand in front of Kimberly and refuse to let her pass. He blocked her way, and then slowly crept closer and closer to her, until, she was so frightened of him, she'd start to cry.

All the while Bill was laughing and taunting. "What's the matter, *baby?* What are you looking at? What are you so scared of?"

I remember one Christmas Day that turned terrible.

I invited my family over to our house for Christmas dinner — my Mother and stepfather, my sister, Shirley, and her children. The kids and I were so excited.

A real family Christinas!

I could hardly wait to be with them again.

At first, even Bill acted like he was looking forward to having a merry day. It *was* Christmas after all. But as the day wore on, his mood started to change.

After opening our presents and spending some time admiring every new trinket, the kids and I went to get dressed for the day. We were laughing together, singing, and having a generally jolly time.

When the kids and I were satisfied with ourselves, we began preparing for our special guests. Kim and Chris had the job to pick up the living room. Keely agreed to set the table. And I went directly into the kitchen to start cooking all my family's favorites.

I was humming around the kitchen, feeling very satisfied with the moment, when I heard Bill shouting at Kim. "Hurry up," he barked. "Get rid of this mess and get out of here. I'm trying to watch TV, for god's sake!"

I stopped what I was doing, and looked over at Keely. She glanced back at me with an expression of pure disappointment.

Now what! What did we do wrong this time?

The kids and I tried to stay out of his way and let him calm down. But without saying so, we were all getting pretty worried.

If he's mad, he'll start screaming again. What's he going to do at dinner? What's grandma going to think?

By the time my family arrived, Bill was in such a foul mood he didn't even look up from the TV to say 'hello'. He just sat there motionlessly — with his arms crossed and a scowl on his face, staring at the television.

Our guests tried to act like they didn't notice anything unusual. But Bill's behavior was impossible to ignore.

There was no doubt in anyone's mind that Bill was purposely putting on a scene. He was doing his best to threaten our celebration with his intense, silent distance.

But we didn't know why. It made everyone uncomfortable and terribly anxious — especially me and the kids because we knew from experience how ugly things could get.

I was scared and angry that Bill was trying to spoil our Holiday. But I didn't know how to stop it. In a very real sense I allowed Bill to take control.

Pretending everything was just fine, we all avoided the living room. Instead, everyone congregated in the kitchen where I was putting the finishing touches on dinner.

While I cooked, the kids helped put dishes on the table. My Mother, sister, and I talked nonstop — filling each other in on what was happening in our lives since the last time we'd seen each other. It felt good to have them there...safer somehow.

Dinner was almost ready, and I was wondering whether to announce to Bill that we were ready to eat, or to just leave him alone. It was really a losing choice — I knew he'd be angry either way.

But before I could figure out what to do, Bill appeared in the kitchen doorway. He just stood there silently glaring at us until he was sure he had our attention. And then he literally erupted!

"This is my house," Bill screamed, "and I can't even get a word in edgewise."

He looked directly at me and started to move closer to where I was standing. Then in front of the kids and my family, Bill shouted into my face, "Who told you to invite your whole god-d----family over here anyway? Get them out of here. Now! And tell them never to come back."

Having accomplished his goal, Bill turned and left the kitchen. I was stunned. The kids and I froze. This was totally unexpected!

Everyone was so embarrassed — it was a terribly uncomfortable situation. There was nothing to say. There was nothing else to do but silently watch my family pack up and leave.

I was furious, hurt, and scared. Bill's manipulative, ugly words... the ruined Holiday...and the kids disappointed faces haunted me.

But the incident was never mentioned. Bill never apologized. I never complained.

Today I wonder why I couldn't see how useless it all was.

Why didn't I protest? Where was my pride? There was no joy! What was I hoping to accomplish?

I'd been here before.

Why didn't I recognize the warning signs? Why did I allow him so much control in my life?

Bill was incredibly dominating. More and more he was treating me like a prisoner in my own home.

Gradually, Bill simply took over altogether. I didn't know *anything* about our family finances. Bill switched all of our bills into his own name, and he put his office address on all our house accounts.

I had no idea how much money he made...if we were in debt... or if we had any savings reserved for emergencies. Bill cashed his paycheck before he came home every Friday, and then he gave me just enough money to cover groceries and Christopher's medical expenses.

I wasn't allowed to drive the car, so I walked everywhere. I bundled up little Chris, set him in his wagon, and off we'd start to the doctor's office, the grocery store, the drug store, and anywhere else we needed to go — no matter how far away it was.

In one year we were forced to move four times because Bill didn't pay the rent on time. But still I was too frightened to complain. I didn't know how Bill would respond. In the back of my mind I was afraid that if he got angry enough, he could really hurt me or the kids.

Bill was changing for the worse. He became more distant... angrier...paranoid...impulsive. His moods and behaviors were so inconsistent, we never knew what he would do next.

But out of fear I did nothing.   And as a result, things started to disintegrate quickly.

Threats

Bill made certain to let me know that my fears were well-founded. A day didn't end that he hadn't screamed nasty expletives at me, or told me how much he hated me...how stupid I was... or what a worthless wife I'd become.

And sometimes at night, after I was asleep, he wrote filthy, threatening messages and taped them to the bathroom mirror. In one way or another, each scribble sent the same message..."I hate you, Connie. I despise the sight of you."

On a really bad morning there would be tens of notes taped all over the house. The kitchen...living room...hallways...even the front door could be covered with little pieces of paper containing Bill's hateful words of anger.

One morning, I got up and went into the living room and couldn't believe what I found. The front door was covered with curse words — each one paired with my name.

It was a horrible forecast.

I ran to the kitchen with tears running down my face.

I can't let the kids see this!

I grabbed the strongest cleanser I could find. I scrubbed and scrubbed until every part of Bill's message was gone.

The words had been removed from the door. But they would never be erased from my memory.

confusion

I think I became so compliant, I lost what little faith I had in myself. When I read those notes, I actually started to believe them.

I was so depressed and tired of worrying, I let Bill convince me that he was right. I lived each day reminding myself — *you really are worthless!*

At night when Chris was asleep and the girls were gone, I escaped the only way I knew how. I drank...and I drank.

Vodka— what a friend it was! After a little one-on-one conversation with my precious bottle, I felt better. Things didn't look so gloomy. I could finally relax.

Sometimes I sat by myself in the dark and let myself imagine that tomorrow would be different. I would wake up and Bill would love me.

It felt good to make believe. But it never happened the way I imagined.

Reality doesn't conform to anyone's drunken dreams. Instead of rekindling a loving relationship with my husband, the exact opposite trend began one very real afternoon.

Chris and Kimberly were playing in Chris's bedroom, and I was sitting at the kitchen table when Bill came home. I heard him hang up his coat in the hall closet, and then he hollered, "Connie, I'm home. Where are you?"

Well, that in itself was unusual. Normally, Bill didn't have any sort of greeting for me except a sideways scowl as he settled into his chair with the evening paper.

What's up with him today? Maybe he's finally going to try and be a part of this family again!

"I'm in the kitchen, honey," I yelled back. "How was your day?" I continued with new eagerness.

I guess I expected to be met with a hospitable response given his cheery greeting. But when Bill came around the corner, he was anything but hospitable or cheery.

Bill was so angry his face looked disformed. His features were tight and drawn. His eyes were wide open...bulging. His neck was strained.

Bill's posture reminded me of an animal poised — a predator!

I was so surprised with this transformation, I stood up and started toward him. I never expected what happened next.

When I walked within his reach, Bill lunged forward and grabbed me. He started slugging me...slapping...pinching...twisting my arms. "My day can go to hell!" he muttered between clinched teeth, "And you can go right along with it!"

Even though I was taken off-guard, somehow I managed to keep my senses. I knew I couldn't fight back and win. Bill was over six feet tall and weighed at least 200 pounds. So I quit struggling with him.

When Bill sensed that I was giving up, his grip loosened a little. In that split second, I wiggled out of his grasp and ran.

I was screaming at the top of my lungs hoping that Kimberly would hear me. "Kim, get Chris into the bathroom and lock the door!" I yelled. "Do it now!"

Thank goodness, she heard me and acted quickly. I heard the bathroom door slam shut.

Bill was in an uncontrollable rage...possessed...overcome with terrible anger. I knew I was running for my life.

With Bill only a few feet behind, I ran through the bedroom door. I whirled around quickly, and with all my might tried to push the door closed in his face — but I was too late!

Bill grabbed my shoulders, pulled me into the room, and pushed me down on the bed. He was silent now...no words...just total rage.

Trying to protect myself, I curled my body into a ball and buried my face in a pillow. But Bill's strength seemed almost superhuman. No matter how I struggled, he overpowered me.

Bill rolled me over and I closed my eyes tight so I didn't have to see into his crazed, wild eyes. He pulled my legs straight and straddled them so I couldn't move.

The pain went on and on.

Bill acted like I was an old doll he was trying to destroy. With one hand, he punched me in the stomach...slapped my face...and pulled my hair. The other fist he used to sock my upper arm until I was sure it was broken.

The pain was terrible. There are no words to describe the fear. I knew I was going to die.

But it wasn't that thought that scared me most. During those awful moments I was most frightened for my children.

Can they hear what's happening? Do they know?

What will Bill do to them? Will he kill them too? Please, Kim, stay with Chris! Keep the door locked!

After what seemed like an eternity, I began to notice that the impacts seemed to be less harsh.

Is *he going to stop?*

I recall wondering if my body was just numb, or if Bill was getting tired. I hoped with all my heart that the latter was true.

I waited for a chance to escape. Silently I waited and planned my strategy. Never in my life have I been more alert than I was during those brief minutes.

My opportunity came and I moved quickly. Either Bill's anger was subsiding, or he had simply worn himself out — I don't know which. But for a split second, I felt his grip around my legs loosen.

This is it! Move now! Go!

I ground my knee into his groin with such force, Bill let go of me. Almost as though it was simultaneous action, I rolled to the side of the bed, threw myself over the side, and took off running down the hallway.

As I ran passed the bathroom door I yelled out at the kids, "Stay there Kim. Don't come out! Don't unlock the door for anything."

Relieved, I heard Kim whimper, "Okay, Mommy."

I could hear Bill starting to come after me, but I didn't take time to look back. I headed straight for the front door. And I got there just in the nick of time. Bill was only a few feet behind me.

I flung the door open, and ran as fast as my feet would carry me into the front yard and across the street toward the nearest neighbor's house. I didn't know whether Bill was still following me, but I had to assume he was. I pounded on our neighbor's door, yelling for help, and crying uncontrollably.

The door was answered almost immediately. There stood two strangers staring at me in total shock and amazement.

I must have looked like a monster. My hair was tumbling around a cracked, reddened face. My eyes were swollen almost closed. My blouse sleeve was askew and torn revealing huge bruises that were already turning blue.

"Help me, please," I sobbed. "Call the police right away!"

Without turning around, I pointed back toward our house and continued with my panicky explanation, "He's going to kill me. And my kids are still inside the house."

The woman behind the screen responded immediately. Turning back inside her house to make the emergency call, she said, "Okay, I'll call the Police. You stay here with her, Adam."

The man nodded an agreement to his wife, opened the door, and stepped out onto the porch. He looked toward our house in an attempt to assess exactly what was going on, and to decide what should be done next.

Staring intently at our house, the man gently and confidently touched my shoulder. I felt as though he was saying, "You can stop running now. You're safe."

With trepidation I allowed myself to follow his gaze. I turned around and tried to focus.

My eyes were so swollen I could barely make out the figure of my husband. Bill was still standing in the doorway of our house, holding the door partially opened. I thought he was staring back at us. He looked as though he was frozen there in mid-flight.

He won't follow me over here. But what about Kim and Christopher. Will he turn on them next?

Please kids, if you've ever obeyed your Mother, do it now. Leave that door locked!

It seemed like time stopped. I was holding my breath. Each of us stood motionlessly, waiting for Bill to make the first move.

As I watched, Bill started to move. Slowly, with such deliberate actions, he moved out of the house and down the porch steps. Without glancing over at us again, he got into the car and drove away.

After I saw Bill's car disappear around the corner, I ran home and went straight to my children. When I reached the bathroom door, I could hear them whispering.

Suddenly the memory of my sister and me cowering together in that little, dark closet flashed back into my mind. I knew my own children were feeling the same fear. They couldn't possibly understand.

I was so sad for them. I never wanted them to have to live through anything like this. Never, never!

Sitting on the floor just outside the bathroom, I knocked gently on the door.

"Kimberly. Chris. It's Mommy," I called quietly. "Everything's okay now. Come on out here with me."

I grabbed my anxious little ones and held them to me for a long time. We cried, and rocked together for a long time. They didn't ask any questions — and I had no answers to offer.

I don't know how much time passed. Kim, Chris, and I were still sitting together in the hallway when I heard voices at the door.

The police responded to my neighbors' call — but they had given them their own address instead of mine. So, still offering to help, Mr. Sanders accompanied the police to our house and knocked on the door.

"It's Adam Sanders with two police officers," he hollered through the door. "Are you all right?"

I took the kids' hands in mine and walked to the door. I guess I expected the officers to take control for me...to protect me and the kids...to make certain Bill could never threaten us again.

But it didn't work out that way.

I couldn't believe my own ears when, after hearing the complete details, the police told me there was nothing they could do!

"Sorry this happened, Mrs. Sharp. But the only advice we have to offer is to try and work out whatever problems you're having with your husband. There's nothing we can do."

I was stunned.

What are they talking about? Work what out? I'm already doing everything I can to make him happy. Nothing works.

I can't even talk to Bill. I don't know why he's doing this.

They've got to be kidding. Are they just going to leave and let him come home and try to kill me again?

There was no question about it. It was *my* problem and I couldn't count on anyone to help me. Somehow or another, I had to figure out what to do.

When Bill came home later that night, he was back to his old, distracted self. There were no signs of the rage. He said nothing to me or the kids. He acted like it was just another day.

coping with the fear

Life resumed in its normal fashion after that fateful day. Bill was gone every day and most every night.

To be honest, I didn't care if Bill never came home. He made us all so anxious. I never let down my guard. I was always suspicious of him — constantly searching his face for warning signs.

It made a stressful home life for the children too — especially for Keely and Kim. They hated it. Every so often I overheard them plotting how they could move out.

But Keely was the only lucky one. Since she was already 18 years old, and out of high school, she could support herself. As soon as she could, Keely found a job and moved away from home. I was sad. But I understood.

Kimberly on the other hand was too young to live out on her own. And she didn't have any other place to go.

So our little foursome turned into a trio. Kim, Chris, and I had each other and no one else.

Then there was the problem of money. If Bill didn't come home, I didn't have any!

One afternoon I found a help-wanted ad in the newspaper. A working Mother was looking for a baby-sitter to take care of her little boy during the day from Monday through Friday.

This is perfect. I love kids. And I can be home for Kim and Chris too.

I called the number and talked with the woman. I could tell from the questions she asked that she was a concerned Mother who just needed to feel secure with her child's care giver.

I didn't have to pretend. I sincerely understood her concerns. I loved my children too and, in her place, I would have pursued the same research. We hit it off immediately.

The very next week, little Max became an eight-to-five member of our family. His Mother dropped him off on her way to work, and picked him up again on her way home.

Between times, we all had a wonderful time together. It felt good to have a little toddler scurrying around the house again.

The word spread, and before long I began receiving calls from other parents who needed child care during the work week. I was thrilled. Soon I had five youngsters to play with...care for...and love.

During that time, Bill's "visits" at home were becoming fewer and farther between — once every other week or so. And even then it was late at night. We never saw each other.

I guess Bill figured if he wasn't going to live in our house, he didn't have to pay for it either! I didn't know that he'd stopped making the rent payments, so I was shocked when our landlord called to tell me I had to either move out or make up for three delinquent months.

I remember standing speechless, with the phone receiver in my hand.

Move, again? No!

I can't make Kim leave her high school and friends. I can't take Chris out of his special training programs.

And what about my Monday-through-Friday care kids?

"Oh my gosh, Mr. Tolar, I had no idea my husband wasn't sending in the rent checks," I started. "He's been out of town a lot lately, and I guess he expected me to pick up that responsibility."

"I will make it up to you right away," I continued. "We'll never be late with another payment — and that's a promise."

I let out a sigh of relief when I heard my landlord's response, "Fine, Mrs. Sharp. Just be sure to keep that promise."

The very next day I scoured the house for every dime I could find. I collected every cent-walked to the bank...and opened a checking account in my name. I was so determined to salvage what was left of our lives.

He can abandon us....but I won't let him throw us out on the street!

It was very hard, but we made it. I managed to pay the landlord our back rent, and keep up with current amounts due.

We lived three years in pretty dire straights. There was never enough money for everything. So, the kids and I learned to make choices. From my child care income we had to conserve for the real necessities — rent... food for the daycare kids, Kim, and Chris...and, of course, my valium, alcohol, and nicotine addictions.

I remember standing in the grocery store wondering whether I should buy peanut butter for lunches or toilet paper. I didn't have enough money for both.

I also remember going to bed at night hoping that Bill was at least paying the utility bills — and wondering what I'd do if he wasn't. Since the statements didn't come to our house, I had no way of knowing, and I was afraid to call the service companies to find out. I knew I couldn't pay for the heat, lights, phone *and* the rent by myself.

I was just hanging on...barely coping. I was drinking more and more to try and forget the worries and fears.

Every day, when the last daycare child left, I poured my first glass of vodka for the evening. By the time Kim and Chris finished their dinner, my one cocktail had usually tripled. And I could laugh again. It made life bearable.

Then after the children were asleep, I sat with my bottle and drink and think...drink and think...until I could barely stand up and maneuver my way to bed. By that point, my dependency on alcohol had grown to five quarts of vodka every week — sometimes more.

But alwayws, my drinking was a very well kept secret. No one knew about my private coping tactics.

Kimberly graduated from high school, and moved on to college. She stayed in close contact. But I still missed her.

Now, we were two.

Abandoned

One afternoon in February 1984, my biggest fear became reality. I answered the doorbell to greet a man from the gas company.

"Mrs. Sharp?" he asked when I opened the door.

"Yes," I responded. "What can I do for you?"

"Unfortunately, you can't do anything for me, Ma'am," he said quietly. "I've been sent to turn off your gas due to an unpaid balance on your account."

He handed me copies of back invoices that proved Bill hadn't paid the gas bill for almost five months. Current unpaid charges added up to more than two hundred dollars! There was nothing to do but stop our service until it was paid.

I felt myself starting to panic.

It's freezing outside, and it's going to stay cold for at least two more months! What am I going to do?

I'll never be able to come up with that much money! How will I keep all these kids warm during the day — and Chris warm at night?

With the service technician waiting for me to say something, I tried to think of every alternative. But there were none. I had no choice but to let him carry out his business.

So there we were — the children and I facing some pretty cold days and nights. I stood in the hallway staring into space...trying to figure out what to do next.

I couldn't call the gas company to plead my case, because I had no way of making the payments. And I had no idea where Bill was, or when he'd come home again!

I felt totally isolated.

The only option I could think of was to ask one of my daycare parents...or maybe my landlord for a loan. But that choice seemed more dangerous than the original problem.

What parent will continue to leave their children with a woman in a freezing, cold house because she didn't pay her bills? And I'm on thin ice with the landlord already — better not push my luck!

It wasn't long after the gas man left our house that afternoon that we began to notice the chill setting in. There was a fireplace in the living room, so I built a fire with some wood Bill had stored in the garage.

By the time parents came to pick up their children, the house was nice and toasty. I explained the fire by saying it was treat for the kids — something fun and different. At all costs, I couldn't let them know what was happening.

They bought my story that first day. But I had to wonder what I was going to do for the days approaching. There wasn't very much wood. And I had no way of getting more.

After the daycare kids were gone, I let the fire die down to conserve what was left of the wood. Chris and I got all bundled up with layers of shirts and sweaters, and played a game that would become our survival ritual for many nights to come.

We pretended that we were "camping out." We ate our dinner by the fire, and sat together rolling newspapers up into tight tubes to get the next day's fire started. When we got too cold we went to bed — no matter what time it was!

I gathered every blanket in the house and piled them all on my bed. Chris and I crawled in under the blankets and stayed there until daylight meant we could afford another fire. I wrapped my arms around my little boy and held him close to keep him warm.

I hardly slept those long, cold nights. I laid awake to be sure Chris was staying warm enough, trying to think of a solution, and watching the clock.

At five o'clock in the morning I got up and built a fire. I needed to warm up the house by the time parents started arriving with their children — I knew I couldn't let them find out about this!

Each morning Chris and I combed the house for anything that would burn! Everything we could find that was nonessential and nonmetallic went into the fireplace on top of our newspaper rolls — wooden spoons...rolling pin...cutting boards... cardboard milk cartons...magazines...picture frames...and wicker things. All of it was burned.

By the fourth morning, Chris and I had used everything we could find in the house. So, I started burning pieces of furniture that were either small enough to fit in the fireplace whole, or that I could disassemble into smaller parts. But I was careful to take things from the bedrooms or kitchen so no one noticed anything missing from the living room!

I kept hoping Bill would come home...find us desperate...and help us. But he didn't.

On the fifth morning I got up at my usual early hour, even though I knew there was nothing left with which to build a fire. I was desperate and scared to death.

It was Friday.

If I can make it through just one more day, I'll have the weekend to find help somehow...just one more day!

I searched through every room to see if Chris and I had overlooked anything flammable. And we hadn't missed a thing!

Then I figured I might as well try the garage once more. So I went out to the garage and searched every corner for something to fuel our fire.

There it is!

Way back in a dark corner I saw an old, wooden orange crate, full of dusty, discolored paper. I almost cried with relief.

I quickly pulled the crate into the house and shoved it in the fireplace. Then I stuck rolls of newspaper all around it, and lit the match.

There was immediate heat! I could hardly believe my good fortune.

Suddenly, as I started to back away from the fire, I realized something was not going well. There were loud cracks...pops...and bright sparks shooting out into the room. It looked and sounded like a mini fireworks display right in my living room!

At once I knew.

I've put too much wood in the fireplace. The wood was too dry. The fire was too hot...too big!

In seconds the fire was out of control. The flames consumed the wood crate almost instantly and were beginning to shoot up and out of the fireplace into the living room.

I ran into the bedroom and pulled Chris out of bed. Holding him close, I grabbed the phone on the bed stand and called the fire department. With as much control as I could muster, I quickly described my emergency and gave my address.

Afterward, Chris and I waited in the hallway, silently watching the flames shooting up...trying to devour the living room wall.

It was six o'clock by then, and I had only one hour before my daycare kids started arriving. I didn't know what to do.

Finally, we heard the sirens and we knew help was on its way. But instead of relief, I wished they would be silent.

What would the neighbors think?

Still holding Chris, I practically leapt to the front door and flung it open. The fire truck was in the driveway and three men were running toward the house pulling a huge water hose.

Without a word, they ran through the door, past Chris and me, and into the living room. In just a few minutes, the fire was gone.

Confidant that the threat had been completely extinguished, one of the firemen turned and walked over to Chris and me. I will always remember him — he was huge and very, very kind.

Christopher was trying to be brave. But he was so frightened, his body was shaking all over.

The fireman bent down, looked into Chris's face, and gently laid his giant hand over my little boy's shoulder. "Don't be afraid," the fireman whispered. "Everything is all right now, son."

Chris looked back up at the big fireman and between sobs he confided his fears like only a child could do. Tears filled my eyes too when I heard his words.

"We don't know where my Daddy is," Chris started. "He won't pay for our heat. It's been really cold in our house for a long, long time. My mommy has to get up early to build a fire every day, but we don't have anything left to burn. We don't have a fire anymore, and now we'll get cold."

The fireman's eyes widened with disbelief. He looked from Christopher to me as if to say — *is this true?*

I was stunned. I didn't say a word, but my silence was the only answer this sensitive man needed.

He knew.

The fireman saved me the disgrace of asking for more explanations. Silently, he squeezed Chris's shoulder, and turned to go.

When the fire fighters were gone, I raced around cleaning up the mess. In under an hour I managed to clean out the fireplace, scrub the black off the mantel, and vacuum the soot out of the carpet. No one would be the wiser, I thought.

But it was cold in the house, and the daycare children would be arriving in ten minutes!

Now what?

With no time to think, I ran and pulled all the books out of a small bookshelf unit tucked under the window in my bedroom. Quickly I pulled the shelves out and disassembled the top from the sides of the unit. They were just the right size!

Carefully, I stacked the shelf pieces of my bookshelf in the fireplace — strategically conserving the rest for later in the day. Then I stuffed some books underneath the wood. It lit easily, and the room was warm again — just in the nick of time.

That was close...too close.

A couple of hours later, the phone rang. It was a representative from the Protective Services office calling.

"Mrs. Sharp, it has come to our attention, from a person who wishes to remain anonymous, that you and your son have been living without heat in your house," he stated matter-of-factly. "Can we help you?"

I didn't think before I responded. "You've called the wrong number," I just blurted out. "Thanks for your inquiry, but no one in *this* house needs a handout!"

Darn that fireman!

Saving face was more important to me than keeping my own child safe and warm. There was only one thought running through my head — *no one can see the way we're living.*

No one can find out!

And no one ever did.

Panic

That same evening, Bill came home for the first time in weeks. Normally, I would have dreaded his return — but this time, I knew he held the only solution. I had to convince him to pay the gas bill and get the heat back in the house.

As soon as Bill walked through the door, it became perfectly clear that something was on his mind. He was completely distracted and more nervous than usual.

I wondered if he'd come home because he'd gotten himself in trouble somehow and needed to lie low. But I knew better than to ask any questions.

In fact, Bill was so distracted that he didn't even sense that the house was fifteen degrees cooler than normal. Nor did he notice more than a few pieces of missing furniture!

Without saying much of anything, Bill methodically walked around the house as though he was looking for evidence of what happened there in his absence. He went through the mail I left in a pile on the counter...checked the phone bills...and rummaged through the clothes and coat closets.

Then, sitting down with the phone bills for a more thorough review, Bill mumbled, "So, what's been going on around here? Have you talked to anybody besides those stupid kids lately?"

"Well, since you asked," I began slowly, "I *did* have two interesting conversations today — one with the fire department and another with the Protective Services office!"

I had Bill's attention immediately. He was staring at me like he'd seen a ghost.

Taking advantage of his obvious alarm, I continued my story. "The gas was turned off five days ago, so every day I've been building fires with anything I could find to stay warm. This morning, the fire got out of control and practically burned the house down! I called the fire department, and I guess they called Protective Services."

For what seemed like forever, there was complete silence. Bill just sat there glaring at me — trying to digest what I was saying. I didn't know exactly what he was thinking about, but I could tell from the tightening muscles in his neck that he was absolutely furious.

"You called *who?*"" Bill screamed, shaking his fist at me. "You stupid, crazy fool!"

Bill literally jumped out of his chair. I thought he was coming after me but instead he went totally out of control — knocking lamps off tables, tipping furniture over, and throwing pictures across the room.

"Don't talk to anyone about me and what I do or don't do!" Bill screamed along with a stream of more instructions. But he was yelling so loudly I couldn't understand half of what he was saying.

As I watched and listened to him, I admitted to myself for the first time that Bill needed help. But I also knew that there was absolutely nothing I could do for him...or even suggest to him. He never listened to me.

In the middle of Bill's rampage, Chris ran into the room and straight over to me. As if trying to protect me, he wrapped his little arms around my legs, and looked over at his Father.

With a stern expression and brandishing his most grown-up voice, Chris shouted a firm demand, "Leave my Mommy alone. Go away!"

Bill whirled around with a shocked expression on his face. I guess he was surprised to hear anyone cross him.

Bill shouted back at Chris, "Shut up, you little idiot! No kid of mine is going to start telling me what to do. This is my house, kid, and I'll come and go as I please. Don't test me, or you'll be sorry!"

"You'll pay for this, you dumb bitch," he yelled on his way out the door. "Never...and I mean never...talk to *anybody about* my business!"

And with that, he was gone again. I had no idea where he was going, but his reaction confirmed my earlier impressions.

He's on the brink of some kind of trouble again.

Thank goodness for me, those suspicions proved right. To avoid any further investigations by authorities, Bill went to the gas company the next morning. He paid up the amounts due, and promised to pay monthly from then on.

Bill's action wasn't out of concern for us. He paid the gas bill to save his own skin. But at that point, I didn't care.

By seven o'clock that Saturday evening, Christopher and I were dancing around the house, clapping with joy. Wonderful, warm air was blowing out of the registers again.

My biggest, most immediate problem had been solved. I knew there would be more challenges, but at that moment, I felt like I could handle just about anything.

Maybe that naivety was a kind of self-defense mechanism I employed. It was too scary and painful to peer into the future and try to predict what might happen there. It was easier to live in the moment. As long as there were no urgent conflicts staring me in the face, I felt okay.

And during the next five months or so, everything was just fine. Bill came home infrequently. And even when he did come, it was usually late at night after Chris and I were asleep. Then he left early in the morning again. There weren't that many opportunities for fights to begin.

Oh, there were a few occasions when Bill came home to stay for an entire weekend. During those extended stays, I was so determined not to incite a confrontation, I tiptoed around the house, waiting on him hand and foot...doing everything I could think of doing to make him happy. *Keep him content* — that was my goal.

And little Chris understood too. He knew to stay out of sight...to play very quietly...no crying...no teasing.

Most of the time, our efforts worked. Bill left as unexpectedly as he'd arrived. Then Chris and I could live again without fear — until the next time.

But, one weekend in July, our strategy failed. Something went very wrong. I don't think there was any way to avoid what happened. To this day, I don't know what triggered the horror.

Bill came home Friday night.

The next morning, Chris and I woke to a beautiful, warm, sunny Saturday. It was a perfect day for a visit to the park.

Following our usual prescription for avoiding conflict, Chris and I whispered over our breakfast cereal, and then just as quietly, tiptoed into his bedroom to get dressed.

Our goal was to get out of the house before Bill woke up. But we weren't quite quick enough.

Chris and I were already to the last step of tying shoes when we heard Bill pulling a coffee mug out of the cupboard.

Darn.. Just five more minutes and we would have been long gone!

Dismayed and disappointed, I whispered into Chris's ear, "Stay here, Sweetheart. I'll be right back."

Assuming as pleasant an expression as possible, I followed Bill into the kitchen. He was sitting at the table staring out the window.

"Hi, there!" I greeted. "It's a beautiful day, huh?"

"Guess that depends on your definition of *beautiful!*" Bill blurted back at me without looking away from the back yard.

"I suppose so," I answered slowly. And then changing the subject, I continued, "Well, honey, unless you need something, Chris and I are headed for the park. We'll be back in a couple of hours."

Leaving his concentrated stare, Bill turned toward me. I remember thinking as I faced him for the first time that he looked so tired...sad... or maybe nervous. I was immediately alarmed. I knew that look.

"Not so fast!" Bill stated emphatically. "We're driving up north to the Slaters' cabin for a cookout today. Get on the phone and find a sitter right away 'cause we'll be late if we don't leave here by noon at the very latest."

I was so confused, I couldn't think of anything to say.

What is this? I had met the Slaters. They lived a few houses down, across the street.

But we weren't friends or even social acquaintances. Why are we going to their cabin for a cookout?

Sensing my unexpressed confusion, Bill offered the explanation. "Mr. and Mrs. Slaters sent me an invitation at work a couple of weeks ago. It's a party for the whole block. Everybody else is going, so we have to show up too."

I stood there searching for an escape route. I couldn't imagine anything worse than spending an entire day with Bill — particularly in front of strangers. Plus the cabin was about two hours or more away. That meant a round trip of at least four hours with him all alone!

God, no!

But, I knew a protest would be futile. In less than one minute, that beautiful Saturday morning turned black.

I felt my stomach tightening, and the fear swelling in my chest. But there was no way out. All I could do was try and get through it.

"Oh, great! Sounds like fun," I lied. "I'll call Kim to see if she can stay with Christopher."

I knew Kim would agree to come if she didn't already have other plans. She loved to spend time with her little brother. And it made me feel a little better knowing that she'd be here with Chris...just in case.

So everything was all set. Here we were — two people who could barely stand the sight of each other, preparing to spend a "fun" day with new friends!

The pretense was ludicrous!

Why are we going through this ridiculous charade? What are you trying to prove? Why won't you just leave me alone?

I spent the next couple of hours in a blur. Almost mindlessly, I changed my clothes, fixed my hair, and put on some makeup. Then I explained the plan to Chris and prepared a casserole for Kim to warm up for dinner. By noon I was ready to go.

We were already an hour or so into our trip before either of us spoke. In fact, I let the silence lull me into a false sense of security.

I can handle this. I'll just keep my mouth shut and get through this.

Out of nowhere, Bill broke the silence. "S---!" he said more to himself than to me. "We were supposed to go under the Highway 31 overpass by now. Where in the hell is it anyway? All I need is to show up late with *you!*"

Ignoring the implied insult, I tried to calm him down. "Welll, hhhonnney," I drawled, "let me look at your map a minute. Maybe it's just farther north than you thought."

Instantly, I knew my offer to help had been a giant mistake. In a split second, Bill reached for me with such force and speed I thought for certain he'd let go of the steering wheel and that he would lose control of the car.

Bill grabbed my arm and started shaking me...first pulling me toward him...and then pushing me away into the car door. He was so strong that his grip lifted me right off the seat.

"I've had it with you!" Bill screamed, "You think you know it all. But you don't know a d--- thing!"

"Sorry!" I pleaded. "I'm sorry. Bill. *Please!*"'

"Shut up you stupid bitch!" he screamed with heightened frenzy. "You're *sorry* all right."

Suddenly, without releasing his grip on my arm, Bill started driving faster and faster. "Get out of the car!" he yelled.

Then, looking straight forward, Bill reached in front of me and tried to pull the door handle. He was pushing me and trying to open the door at the same time. I was pinned in the corner between the door and the seat back.

He kept screaming, "Get out! Do you hear me, you worthless piece of s---? Get out of this f------- car!"

I was crying hysterically, "Stop it, Bill! Please! Stop!" I was petrified. I couldn't fight back.

Then, I remembered a strategy that had worked once before.

Give *up, Connie. It's your only chance.*

So, with every bit of self control I had, I quit crying...quit begging. I made myself go limp, and just sat completely still against the door.

It worked!

As suddenly as Bill's fury began, it ended. He calmed instantly, slowed the car down, and pulled his arm away from me.

Our trip resumed in silence as though there had been no interruption! I couldn't believe it. I was afraid to even breath.

Bill figured out where we'd made a wrong turn and without much of a detour we found the Slaters' cabin. It was at the end of a long, wooded driveway, and I could tell by the number of cars parked along the drive that there were a lot of people there.

Oh, god, how am I going to do this?

As we left the car and approached the cabin, I could hear our neighbors talking and laughing. There was no doubt they were having a good time.

What am I doing here? I almost died an hour ago! This man tried to push me out of a speeding car!

Somehow or another I managed to control myself. I just put one foot in front of the other-plastered a smile on my face...and concentrated on taking deep, regular breaths.

Soon we were part of the happy group, and no one but me seemed the wiser. But the thing I'll never forget was the way Bill transformed from the monster in the car into the friendliest, most amicable "life of the party."

I couldn't believe it. Bill moved through the crowd easily — talking...joking...making friends. He smiled and laughed. He drew people to him so naturally.

I followed him around like a faithful little puppy. I smiled on cue, and shyly created a false presence that announced a quiet, but happy wife.

But underneath, I was a nervous wreck. I wanted to scream out and tell everyone that Bill was a cruel, horrible man.

He tried to kill me, for god's sake!

My stomach was tied in knots. I sat pushing food around my plate, holding back tears until my eyes were stinging and sore.

Behind my placid exterior, there was an internal alarm that wouldn't stop ringing in my ears. I dreaded the trip, but I desperately wanted to get back home.

What's going to happen?

At long last, Bill made the rounds with me in tow, saying goodbye to his newly-found friends. We thanked our hosts, and left for home.

My stomach was sick with fear. But I knew if I could make it home without triggering a recurrence of Bill's anger, everything would be all right.

I knew that he'd drop me off in front of the house and leave at once. I could run into the house and lock the door. I could hug my children.

And then, finally, I could try and forget this horrible night over a couple of drinks in the quiet safety of my dark living room. It sounded like a piece of heaven to me.

And that's just what happened. Bill left as soon as we got home. I remember wondering for the first time as I watched him drive away whether he was on his way to terrorize the life of another woman.

But as quickly as the thought flashed through my mind, I forgot. I didn't really care. I just wanted him gone.

I walked through the door happy to be alive. It was the first genuine smile I had all day.

Chris was already sleeping. I kissed Kimberly as she left, and went straight for my bottle of vodka.

I fixed myself as many drinks as it took to make my body stop aching, and to make the pain in my heart go away. I sat by myself for long, long time that night.

There was an incredible flood of fear, shame, guilt, and anger...

When will he strike again — and how? Will I be prepared?

How did I allow myself to get involved with a man like Bill in the first place! How could I have been so stupid? With my track record, I should have learned my lessons long before now!

I've made the same kind of mess out of my life and the kids' lives as my parents made for me.

Why am I not strong enough to make it stop?

What did I do to deserve this? I've tried to do all the things a woman does for the man she loves, but still I get beaten. Nobody deserves this!

I've learned to live with the marks on my body, but the scars embedded deep down inside me will never heal. No, I won't ever forget.

I will never forget, but at least I've got valium and vodka to deaden the pain. At least I can still make it through the days.

depression

Christopher and I went through the rest of that summer without incident. The daycare kids came every day. And occasionally, Keely and Kim came over for dinner and to play with Chris.

Bill never came home for more than an hour or two — and then it was only to pick up something. He paid little attention to us. I figured my suspicions about Bill having another woman somewhere were true.

I had no friends. And I couldn't tell my Mother what was happening. She'd try to shame me into leaving Bill. And I wasn't prepared for that.

As the autumn season approached, my loneliness turned into full-fledged depression. Not even my vodka and valium were successful at keeping the "edge off" anymore.

One especially lonely night, I was in the bathroom getting ready for my usual evening alone with more than a just "few" drinks, when a thought raced into my head and stuck. There it was — my bottle of valium...and it was almost full. All those tiny pills swallowed at once could be my way out forever!

In a very sick way, I was excited over the thought. It was a kind of release.

I decided right then that I would take an overdose of valium. I didn't know exactly when, but as soon as I could I would end this mess of an existence once and for all.

It was my only way out. It was the only way I knew to escape the pain. I simply didn't want to live anymore...fight anymore.

Taking a long look into the bathroom mirror, I almost gasped at the face looking back at me. The chemicals were taking their toll.

I'd lost so much weight, I didn't make it to 100 pounds even on a heavy day. My skin was grey. And my eyes looked sunken deep in my face — they looked dead...dark.

I stood looking at myself on that dark night and sobbed. I cried until I had no energy left.

Such a terrible mess I was. I hate myself. I hate my life.

When I was all cried out, I left the bathroom and took my bottle of vodka to the picture window in the living room. For as long as I live, I won't forget the anger and despair I felt that night.

I stood alone in that darkened room. I looked up into the sky and began talking to an imaginary listener.

"I know there's no god...there's no heaven...and there's no hell except the one I'm living in," I started. "But, if by some outside chance, there *is* a god, then you listen to me. I hate you. I HATE YOU. I HATE YOU!"

"How could you allow anyone to have such a horrible life?" I went on. "Well, it really doesn't matter because I am going to kill myself anyway and then it won't matter. I mean it. I hate you."

And I really did mean every word. I would make sure to end the pain within the next few days.

Breaking the Cycle

It's Never Too Soon — or Too Late

When a woman's self respect has been destroyed, when she has
been deeply hurt (physically or emotionally) and made to feel
the injury was her own fault, when she risks her own safety or
the well-being of her children just to beg shreds of approval from
someone who cannot or will not provide it — she is caught in a
no-win cycle that will continue to repeat itself until she changes its
course.

She is playing the role assigned to her by her abuser. She has given
her own choices away and empowered her abuser to continue
inflicting pain.

It's time to stop playing that role. It's time to break that cycle and
write your own script. Salvation means learning how to respect
yourself and how to demand respect from every person you choose
as a companion. But first you must truly believe deep in your heart
and soul that you *deserve* that respect just as much or more than
the next person.

Salvation means learning to see that the abusive behavior of
another person is not your fault. You are not to blame. For victims
of abuse, healing comes down to "forgiveness" — forgiving
yourselves.

The process of forgiving yourself is a long — yet sweet — battle.
But when you've chosen to break the cycle by admitting you
deserve to be loved and respected, as soon as you empower
yourself with a commitment to try — you have fought more than
half the battle. Much more.

Two days after promising my own demise, I was wandering around the house in my normal state of blurred depression when I heard a knock at the front door. Opening the door, I greeted a man who I'd met a few months earlier.

I couldn't remember his name at first, but I recalled that he was an acquaintance of Bill's. They had gone to college together years before, and still met occasionally for lunch.

"Hi, Connie," the stranger began, "we met a couple of months ago. I'm Norm — a friend of your husband's. Is Bill home?"

As Norm introduced himself, my memory of him cleared.

Oh, yes! You're the "crazy Christian" who loaned Bill money. You're the guy who talks non-stop about your religious nonsense.

Bill laughs at you and mimics you. You silly fool! Don't you know that Bill's just using you?

the "crazy" Christian

"Hi, it's nice to see you again," I responded with insincere pleasantry. "But, I'm sorry, Bill's not home."

Oh god, this is just great! The last thing I want is a fanatic Christian in my house talking like a maniac about Christ.

But, it was too cold outside to leave him standing on the porch. And I knew I couldn't just say *good bye,* and shut the door in his face.

"Well, come on in, Norm," I said. And holding the door open for him, I tried to bring the visit to a quick conclusion with a simple statement, "Bill's out of town, but I'd be glad to pass on your message when he calls."

To my surprise and despair, Norm didn't pick up on my attempt to cut our discussion short. He just walked right by me into the living room and promptly sat himself down on the couch!

Thinking back, it must have been a comical setting. There I stood with my hand still on the half-opened door looking with wonder at this nutty stranger who had settled quite comfortably in my living room!

Instantly I was alarmed.

Bill was right. This guy is crazy. Now he's going to start in on me with his witnessing nonsense.

He's acting like he plans on staying for a while. Oh, no! I can't take this. How could anybody be so presumptuous to try and talk to total strangers about his belief in Jesus Christ? How dumb!

This is a nightmare! How am I going to get him out of here?

Warily, I walked into the living room to join my unwanted visitor. Sitting across from Norm, I said again, "Would you like me to give Bill a message for you, Norm?"

"Yep," he responded easily, "I need to remind Bill that he owes me some money. I offered to help him out with a loan a few months ago, and Bill promised to pay me back before now."

There was no hint of urgency in Norm's demeanor. And there was no anger in Norm's voice as he continued, "Maybe Bill has just forgotten, but I'd like to talk with him about it soon. Do you know how I can contact him?"

Maybe it was Norm's quiet voice, or his calm, confident face that put me off guard. But for some reason, I suddenly forgot my dislike of this stranger. Before I knew it, I was feeling more relaxed and comfortable.

Listening to Norm talk, I realized that he was a kind and honest man who made a big mistake in trusting my husband. For Norm, I was disappointed. For me, I was embarrassed.

I knew Bill would be furious with me if he ever discovered that I'd confided in Norm. So I tried to explain the situation as well as I could without revealing too much.

"Well, like I said, Bill is out of town," I began slowly, looking straight into my own lap. "And to be perfectly honest, he's *been* away for a long time. I really can't tell you where he his — I don't know. And I have no idea when he'll be home next."

"I'm so sorry this has happened, Norm," I continued, meaning every word. "If I had the money to pay you back, I would. But I'm afraid I don't."

When I was finished, I looked up at Norm expecting to see angry distrust in place of his previously calm countenance. But there was no sign of disturbance there.

Norm was silent. He sat very still with that same kind and confident expression on his face. Then he looked deep into my eyes and seemed to be searching for more — a better understanding.

But I couldn't meet his intense gaze. I was afraid he really could see the truth. All I could do was look at the floor and hope that this would end soon.

Finally, Norm broke the awful silence. "Connie, it's all right. Don't worry about this. I'll work it out with Bill one way or another."

"But now I'm wondering about you — since your husband seems to be away more than he is here, are you and your little boy okay? Do you have everything you need? Do you need help with anything?"

The concern I heard in Norm's voice surprised me so much I almost forgot to keep my secrets. I wanted to rush over to him and tell it all.

Help? Yes, Norm, please help us!

But I caught hold of myself in time and answered Norm's inquiry as cautiously as possible.

"Thank you," I said through a false smile, "but, no, I don't need anything. Christopher and I are just fine."

Thinking my answers would end this uncomfortable confrontation, I stood up and headed toward the door, expecting Norm to do the same.

But to my dismay, he wasn't budging. Norm just continued to sit on my couch, looking at me with that same intense expression that was beginning to really make me nervous.

As I turned to face my stubborn visitor, my surprise must have been apparent. A little apologetic smile appeared on Norm's face as he stood and put on his coat.

"Well, Connie," he said, "I guess that about does it. It's been nice to see you again, but I'd better be going now."

Then Norm dropped a note on the coffee table and said, "Here's my phone number. Just tell Bill to give me a call when you speak with him, will you?"

I nodded, and with a smile I tried to reassure Norm. "Sure," I said, "that's the least I can do."

Reaching to open the door for my exiting guest, I couldn't believe my ears when this persistent stranger continued talking!

"May I ask you just a couple of questions before I leave?" Norm asked.

"Yes. What?" I responded, hoping my exasperation wasn't too evident.

Norm put his hands on my shoulders and replied, "Connie, if you haven't already put your faith in the Lord Jesus Christ, I'd like you to know that He can be a wonderful, never-ending source of love and help if you will only call on Him. *Do* you believe in Jesus Christ as your personal savior? Do you understand His promises? Do you pray every day for help and guidance?"

I don't think I even responded right away. I only remember staring back at Norm in disbelief.

Oh my gosh, what a lunatic! I cannot believe you're actually talking to me like this ~ making these fanatical claims and asking me such stupid questions.

But keeping my senses, I smiled knowingly. "Yes, I've believed in God since I was a very young girl. And, yes, prayer is a regular practice in this home," I mouthed dishonestly. "But thanks again for your concern."

At that point, I would probably have admitted to being a nun! I would have told Norm just about anything to get him to leave.

"That's great! I'm so glad," Norm answered quietly, but I could tell that he wasn't completely convinced. Then he handed me a book, and finally appeared to be leaving.

"Here, I brought a new Bible for you," Norm said. "And I took the liberty to highlight some of my favorite passages, hoping you and Bill might enjoy them too."

"See you later, Connie," Norm said as he walked through the door. "And remember to call me anytime for any reason!"

I stood with my ear against the door, listening to his departing footsteps until I was certain Norm was really leaving. Then I locked the door and literally ran to the living room window to confirm that his car was actually pulling away from the curb.

Absentmindedly I threw the Bible down on the coffee table as I sank into the couch. I was so relieved that Norm was gone. But as I sat by myself reviewing Norm's words in my mind, I felt an odd, lingering anxiety.

Man, oh man — this guy is certifiable! He might be a nice guy if he wasn't such a crazy Christian!

How does anyone have the guts to go from talking about your husband owing them money to nonsense about personal relationships with Jesus Christ... prayer habits...and Bible verses? Now that takes nerve!

So, Connie, if he and his Bible verses are just some kind of craziness, why are you getting so upset?

I don't know why, but Norm makes me nervous — and that's for d--- sure! After this, I'm going to look before I open the door. If Norm ever comes back here, I just won't answer.

Shaking myself back into reality, I got up, fixed myself a short shot of vodka, and continued my aimless wandering around the house. I felt totally exhausted. All I wanted to do was fall into a deep, deep sleep and forget that this day had ever dawned.

But as much as I wanted to, I knew I couldn't just go back to bed. Chris would be home soon and he'd expect some playtime and dinner.

So I opted for an alternate plan. I'd do what I often did to take my mind off my troubles — clean out and reorganize closets. I picked the top shelves in my bedroom since they hadn't been touched for years, and that was just the time-consuming challenge I needed.

Pulling a chair into the closet, I climbed into position to reach the highest, darkest corner. I remember laughing a little as I tried to imagine what hidden and forgotten "treasures" I'd find.

Extending my arm above my head as far as it would stretch, I began grasping and pulling at things. I couldn't believe how many boxes and bundles had accumulated up there.

What is all this stuff?

All of a sudden, something fell off the shelf, hit the top of my head, and fell to the floor.

Ouch! What in the heck was that?

It almost seemed as though the object — whatever it was — "jumped" off the shelf on purpose!

I crawled down from the chair to search for my mystery attacker. As I looked down, my heart skipped a beat. There on the floor lay an old, long-forgotten Bible!

Stunned, I picked it up and read the title. I saw "Living Bible" written in big letters.

"Living" all right — this thing definitely has a life of its own!

Then I started to shake.

Where did this come from? Two Bibles in one day!

I sure don't ever remember seeing this Bible. It isn't mine or the children's. And it certainly doesn't belong to Bill!

As I stood there wondering, a very disturbing explanation came to mind.

Maybe there really is a God. And maybe He's trying to get my attention. Maybe I should read some of this book!

Now, I'm the one who's crazy. But what the hell, I don't have anything to lose, that's for sure.

And besides, I'm really good at keeping secrets. No one has to know I'm actually reading the Bible.

a *truth that heals*

Leaving my chair-ladder right where it was, I left my project and walked back into the living room. I felt very strange walking through my house, staring at this new discovery.

I wanted more than anything to hope. But my thoughts were full of doubt.

Not having the slightest idea where to begin, I just opened the Bible and started to read. I read and read and read. Sometimes I read the same chapter over and over. And then I flipped to a new spot and begin again.

I couldn't stop. I didn't want to stop. I don't know how long I stayed alone and absorbed. Hours.

The words made so much sense to me. My heart reveled in the truth. The messages were clear...comforting...wonderful.

> "I KNOW THE PLANS I HAVE FOR YOU," SAYS THE LORD. "THEY ARE PLANS FOR GOOD AND NOT FOR EVIL. I WANT TO GIVE YOU A FUTURE FULL OF HOPE."
>
> "WHEN YOU PRAY, I WILL LISTEN. YOU WILL FIND ME WHEN YOU LOOK FOR ME. I AM HERE ALWAYS, AND I WILL BE WITH YOU, IF YOU LOOK FOR ME WITH ALL YOUR HEART."

Jeremiah 29: 11-13

I was filled with incredible hope. I wanted with every fiber of my being to claim these promises for myself.

But I was frightened — scared to believe that an unseen presence could really be so all-knowing...powerful...wonderful...loving. And, most of all, I was afraid to believe that God was actually speaking to *me* with these words.

I didn't want to invest all my hopes in just another false promise. I knew I would never recover from a disappointment like that.

As I sat holding my Bible — the hopes and fears inside me waging their own battle.

Can this be true? How do I know?   What will happen to me if I surrender to this?

The tears wouldn't stop. Everything that had previously been "real" to me seemed incredibly confused now. I felt nothing but a bungled mess of intense emotions — hope and relief fighting against doubt and fear.

I will always remember searching the same sky into which just a few nights earlier I shook my fists in anger and screamed hateful words to an unknown god.

I cried out, "Is this true? If you're really there, God, I will believe in you for the rest of my life! I will. I promise. But I'm scared. I've made too many mistakes before. I need to know for sure!"

Very, very gradually, I began to feel a wonderful, comforting peace seep inside my mind and body. It was a gentle warmth filling me, replacing my fears and confusion. It was an all-encompassing peace of mind — strong... knowing...calming.

As I stood alone, my tears and shaking subsided. And then, just as clearly as if someone was whispering into my ear, I heard the words I so desperately wanted to hear...

"Connie, I love you. I am the Way and the Truth. I am the Light of Life. I have been waiting to heal you." "Don't be afraid any longer. You are mine now. I have loved you since the beginning of time and I will love you forevermore."

In that instant I claimed the truth that I have lived with every day since.

Jesus Christ lives! He is God — the Creator and Master of our world. And He loves me!

On March 14, 1985, I fell on my knees, and talked to God for the first time in my life. All the love I had left to give I offered into the arms of Jesus Christ.

I begged for forgiveness, and new strength. I pleaded with Jesus Christ to help me overcome all the loneliness, fear, and addictions that plagued and controlled my life.

At that moment, my living room filled with the presence of a thousand angels. I sensed their light...their rejoicing...and the perfect, eternal love of God. I was absolutely and completely filled with the Spirit of God.

I felt alive for the first time in my life. I have never felt such warmth and hope. I knew my life would be different from that moment on. I would walk with Christ.

Old things would become new.

As quickly as God promised, He delivered. My cries from fear and confusion were replaced with tears of sheer delight.

I got up off my knees and ran into the bathroom. I couldn't wait to look at myself the mirror.

I feel so new...like a totally different person. Do I look different too?

Yes! There was my reflection staring back at me through clear, sparkling, smiling eyes. All signs of gloom and despair and darkness vanished. I was radiant!

With every nerve, I felt an incredible surge of energy. I was so excited...so happy...so anxious to know what would happen next.

I ran from the bathroom back into the living room hoping to feel the presence of my celebrating angels once again. They were still there!

Now that I think back, it's probably good that I was home alone — anyone would have thought me a lunatic! I laughed and danced around the house — all the while thanking God for His miracle and promising my trust and obedience in return.

I collected every valium pill, every cigarette, and every ounce of vodka I'd stashed and flushed it all down the toilet.

It was the first time in my life that I felt unafraid. I felt absolutely "crazy" with a fresh sense of life.

I had finally found *someone to love me.*

changes

My life changed that afternoon. I didn't understand why God wanted *me* — a miserable, alchoholic, drug addict who had made one horrible mistake after another.

Why would God want someone who consistently chose to make such a mess out of life?

But, even with that wonder, I had no doubt that Jesus Christ really *did* want me, and best of all, He had forgiven each and every one of my mistakes.

Christ eliminated my shame. He took away my guilt.

From that afternoon, I had a new outlook on life. I found the confidence, security, and peace I'd been searching for unsuccessfully my entire life. I felt a wonderful, personal strength building inside myself in the knowledge that Jesus Christ would love me...protect me...and guide my way through whatever would come.

I lost the intense need to search for affection. Christ became my constant companion. I was settled in spirit, mind, and body.

The fears...confusion...anxiety...and panic vanished. My thoughts became clear and focused. Literally overnight, my mental and physical addictions disappeared — and I have never felt the need for valium, alcohol, or cigarettes since then.

Best of all, I learned to see myself as Christ does — through eyes full of boundless love and forgiveness. Instead of constantly carrying a heavy burden of self-blame and guilt, my heart was filled with the incredible miracle of Christ's grace and mercy.

I could stop shaming myself into believing that all the pain and abuse was somehow really my own fault. I could stop believing that I was a nasty, worthless woman who *deserved* the hurt.

Suddenly, through Christ's offer of unconditional love, I could see my own value. It was then, and still is, the most wonderful confidence.

a new-found courage

In spite of my new excitement, there was a dismal thought that lingered in my mind. I knew Bill was bound to come home eventually, and I didn't know what I'd do when that day came!

How will I deal with Bill? He'll never change. He will always be angry.

But how do I tell him everything's different now...that I refuse to be his victim...that he is not allowed to terrorize me any longer? He won't listen. He won't stop. What will happen then?

I didn't have long to wonder. Bill came home just one week following Norm's visit.

As I watched Bill's car pull into the driveway, I was filled with both fear *and* anticipation. I was anxious to tell him about my new life in Christ, but I was unsure and frightened over what his reaction would be.

I waited for what seemed like an eternity, almost afraid to breathe. When Bill finally walked through the door, I met him with a confidence that could only have come from God.

"Hi, I'm glad you're here because I have some important news for you," I blurted out at once. And before Bill could even respond, I went on. "My life has changed, Bill. I'm a Christian now. I believe that Jesus Christ is my Savior!"

"Oh, for god's sake, Connie. What are you jabbering about now?" Bill barked back as he walked toward me. "Get real. You're the dumbest bitch I've ever known. I leave for a few days, and you get religion!"

Bill searched my face as though he really did think I'd lost my senses. And as I watched him approach, I was immediately on guard. My muscles tightened. I couldn't stop the fear.

Oh, God. It's happening all over again. I can't stop him!

No, Connie. Stop shaking. Calm down. Tell him everything's different now. Make him believe you!

Then with Bill standing directly in front of me, I somehow found the courage to respond. *"I'm* not the one with the problem here, Bill. *You* are!" I said quietly, but firmly.

Bill's face revealed nothing but total disbelief. So, I continued with my explanation.

"Your friend Norm came here last week to ask for the money you owe. I told him I didn't know where you were."

"Norm talked with me about Jesus and left a Bible to read. I read it and I'll believe it until the day I die. I am Christ's child now. He loves me, and He'll take care of me from now on! You can't hurt me anymore. You can't make be feel guilty and stupid!"

Instantly, Bill lunged and pushed me back against the wall. Putting his hands around my face, he started shaking my body and banging my head against the wall. His eyes were full of fury.

Bill screamed the same words over and over again. "I don't give a s--- who or what you believe in. I told you *never* to talk to *anyone* about me. Do you hear me, bitch? *Never talk to anyonel"*

Every time my head hit the wall it felt like it would explode. My body was limp. I was crying uncontrollably. I wondered if Bill would stop before he killed me!

Say something, Connie! Anything to make him stop. Don't fight. Protect yourself.

"I'm sorry, Bill. I'm sorry," I cried. "Stop. I'll never talk to anyone again."

"You're d--- right, you won't!" Bill yelled with a final, excruciating slap across my mouth. "If you do, I'll make sure it's the last time you open your stupid mouth!"

And with that, Bill was gone. He just turned around and left as quickly as he'd arrived.

As the door slammed shut, there was a split second of relief. But then the old terror moved in. I covered my throbbing head with my arms and sunk to the floor — a heap of pain, tears, and confusion.

Pounding my fist against the door, I screamed accusations, "Where are you now, Jesus? Why did You let this happen? You promised to take care of me! But nothing has changed. Have you forgotten?"

Then, all at once, I stopped. Through the silence came soft, loving answers as I recalled the words of Christ...

"Be still, Connie, and know that I am God. I am here with you now. I will show you the way and I will stay by your side."

In that instant I knew something *had* changed. Huddled alone in the corner of my front hall, I sensed a brand new strength in *myself.* This wasn't the some old scenario repeating itself, I had changed! I had an *omnipotent* partner to love me and guide me!

It seemed as if I'd just discovered a reservoir of inner strength that never existed before.

I am bruised... but not broken. I am afraid... but not conquered.

I remember sitting motionlessly and completely absorbed in these amazing, new feelings of confidence. Christ was there with me. His spirit filled me...surrounded me...comforted me. Even as I looked at my yellowing arms and felt my eyes starting to swell shut, I reveled in the strange, but reassuring sense of hope and courage.

Right there and then I made the promise to myself...to Christopher... and to God above that, no matter how frightening the obstacles, I was ready and willing to find a way out. The abuse...the lying...the fear... it all must stop.

My perspective of things changed dramatically. I saw myself, and Bill, and our so-called life together much differently than before. I no longer felt the constant need to seek Bill's affection. I no longer dreaded his obvious disapproval.

Maybe it was the assurance of God's unconditional, never-ending love...maybe it was knowing that my weaknesses and mistakes were forgiven...and maybe it was believing in Christ's promise to help... but my willingness to remain a cowering, helpless victim trapped in an abusive lifestyle vanished.

Oh, I was still very much afraid of Bill's angry outbursts and heavy blows. But, for the very first time, I realized that *his* uncontrollable behavior was not *my* fault. I was not responsible for *his* sick, volatile anger. I had done nothing to cause it, and I couldn't do anything to stop it.

My only regret was that I had put up with the awful threats and stifling fear for too long. I knew during those moments that the time had finally come — it was my responsibility to find a way out...and quickly!

At the time, I had no idea *how* I would manage such immense changes. From every vantage point, the prospect of changing my life looked like an absolute impossibility. There were no obvious solutions or alternatives. I had no support system of any kind.

But in spite of the scary and seemingly insurmountable obstacles, I was resolved to make big changes. I put every ounce of trust I could muster in Christ's promise to guide and protect me and little Chris.

It was the most important commitment I have ever made.

Starting Over

A Conscious Choice

The prospect of starting over is immensely intimidating. The process seems impossible. The challenges insurmountable. There are too few choices and way too many unknowns.

It's easy to fall back on the old excuse that "some things just can't be changed." Sometimes, knowing what to expect — although it hurts — seems a lot safer than facing a string of tomorrows full of strangeness. And it's tempting to believe that eventually things will just work themselves out on their own.

But for most of us, things just don't work out for the better by themselves. To begin a new life, *you* must be the catalyst. *You* must make the choices. *You* must make the changes.

But you don't have to head into a new future alone. When you're able to see yourself as a loving, deserving person, others will be there to agree with you. When you are ready to take one step after another, others will be there to help.

Your salvation journey begins inside your own heart. Make a conscious decision to be healed. And above all, have faith in God's promise to never leave you alone.

When a person has been "trapped" in a destructive life pattern (like I was) for so long, it is an incredible experience to suddenly recognize that there's another option — a way out! And it's even more mesmerizing and uplifting to actually feel as though you have the *power* to follow through with your resolve...to *instigate* a series of changes...to move ahead in a *different direction* in order to bring about a new and happier life.

In fact, hundreds of books have been written describing the immense personal power that comes from a mixture of sincere resolve, positive thinking, and self-confidence. The essence of the message — we can find a way to accomplish just about anything as long as we put our minds to it!

I agree, but only halfheartedly! It's true...we are our own masters!

But, from experience, I'd like to add a very critical warning — the vision of a wonderful, new life and the resolve (no matter how strong and confident) to find it is *only* the very first, and often easiest, step of a very tough climb.

Yes, we all have to take that first step. 'I can and I will' decisions are needed to forge ahead. But never, never let the "heady" feelings of anticipation veil the plain truth that there will be some tough challenges on the path to change.

Actually taking the steps to end the old and begin a new life is much more difficult and frightening than simply making a mental promise to do so. Remember — you may have changed, but chances are the people and circumstances around you have not! And it will be your challenge to decide what the new you does with the old reality of things...and how.

Face it! In some cases, there will be resistance. There will be questions without obvious answers.

Where do I go from here? How do I avoid falling back into the same old patterns that got me into trouble in the first place? I know where I want to leave. But, where am I headed...and how do I get there?

And, unfortunately, there are no road maps or step-by-step instruction booklets.

At the very least, to really make abrupt turns in life that will affect lifelong changes, one must have an incredible amount of courage and determination. But above all, it requires faith — *faith* in the knowledge that a solution really does exist somewhere, and that you have the ability to find it!

For me, the source of that faith had to be something much, much bigger than *all* of my own inner resources.

My confidence has come solely from the Lord Jesus Christ...His undying love for me...His answers to prayer...and belief in His deity over all creation.

answered prayers

I suppose everyone, for one reason or another, has been forced to look *reality* straight in the face, and admit to staring at a pretty bleak picture. I know I did. And it was a startling experience.

I had allowed life to get so messed up. And so not to accept responsibility for the mistakes, I lived each day trying to pretend none of it existed.

I was an expert at avoiding a good long look at the circumstances surrounding me. Every time a tiny glimpse of the truth began to rear its ugly face, a nip of vodka or a valium tablet could erase the vision — or at least soften the edges.

Then, almost overnight, I found myself without an escape route. The vodka was gone. The valium was gone. Suddenly, all the harsh ugliness of reality became very clear.

I remember thinking —

Well, this is it, Connie. This isn't a pretty picture. There's not a whole lot to work with here!

And the truth of the matter was, things *did* look pretty hopeless!

But, for the first time in my life, I felt empowered. I had a mission. Although I had no idea where or how to begin, I was determined to take control of my life instead of trying to escape from it.

For several days after that last encounter with Bill, I woke up in the morning feeling like a visitor in my own life! The thoughts and behaviors that had been such practiced, familiar parts of my daily life now seemed foreign.

Even though nothing *around* me had really changed — I *had* changed. I felt like a different person surrounded by a life that used to belong to someone else.

Nothing was as it had been. Everything was new. I felt free and content. I was happier than I'd ever been in my entire life.

For a while I was content simply wallowing in this new-found joy. I suppose you could say I just took a vacation from thinking about the future and what I was going to do about it.

Chris and I spent day after day in our own little happy fantasyland. We sang along, as loudly as we could, with Christian music on the radio. We read the Bible together. We laughed. And we prayed.

But even through this brief timeout, worries lingered in the background. Bill was bound to return — and when he did, the abuse would resume. My biggest concern (even more frightening to me than the surety of physical pain) was wondering how I would keep myself from responding to his threats in the old, helpless, self-destructive ways.

With all my heart I didn't want that to happen. But, no easy answers came to mind.

Where do I go? What can I do? How do I begin?

There were two things I knew for certain... My immediate future would present some very difficult challenges. And I knew I couldn't face them alone. I needed to find help somewhere — a support system.

I decided that the most obvious first step was to find a church... a place that I could call home. At least on Sunday, I wouldn't be alone.

There's safety in numbers, after all!

At a church, I could learn more about Jesus Christ and His purpose for my life. The idea of being surrounded by a group of people who shared my love of Christ was incredibly inviting to me.

The more I thought about it, the more excited I became.

I would start this Sunday.

The goal became a sort of personal obsession — a real-life symbol that I was really beginning to take control. I had taken the first step!

As I look back at that decision, it seems like a pretty simple step. But at the time it really was a huge leap! I hadn't stepped inside a church — nor had I wanted to — for years. This was quite a drastic change.

But precisely for that reason, I didn't have the slightest idea which church to attend. I remember that Friday afternoon, skimming through the phone book trying to find a familiar name. I prayed for something to become evident. But nothing happened.

As I sat at the kitchen table wondering what to do, my musing was interrupted by the doorbell. When I opened the door, my heart skipped a beat. It was Norm!

Why hadn't I thought of that? Norm would know what to do. Oh, thank you, Jesus, for this "crazy," wonderful Christian!

I was so excited, I practically yanked Norm into the house. And without a proper greeting I set out after my goal.

"Hi, Norm. I'm so glad to see you. I have to find a church, but I don't know where to start. I don't know a thing about any of them. May Chris and I go to church with *you* Sunday?"

Norm laughed and nodded. "Well, 'Hi' to you too, Connie! I go to Immanuel Reformed Church, and I think you and Chris would like it too. But, unfortunately, I'm leaving town for the weekend. I just stopped by on my way out to say 'Hi', and see if you need anything."

Sensing my disappointment, Norm quickly continued, "But it doesn't matter whether I'm here or not — you and Chris can go anyway! The church is only a mile or so away from here. And you don't have to worry about going alone or feeling out of place. It's a really friendly group. There will be plenty of people ready to welcome you."

Yes. Yes. I can do that! This is perfect.
Prayer number one — Answered.

I gave Norm a big thank-you hug, assured him that he had just given me the *only* thing we needed, and sent him on his way.

"Thanks, Norm," I hollered with a wave goodbye, "have a good time. Call me when you get back."

Christopher and I could hardly wait for Sunday morning. Through the rest of Friday, we tried to imagine what *our* new church would be like. We wondered about the things we'd learn there. We dreamed about new friends.

We planned our first church visit very carefully. Saturday I'd call the church and find out what time to be there. And, then, since we'd probably have to walk, Chris and I would be sure to get ready at least an hour before.

Just briefly we thought about the possibility of Bill showing up and allowing us to drive the car to church. But, neither Chris nor I wanted to discuss that option for very long. We both agreed that it would be better to just walk.

The anticipation felt so good. Without actually saying so, we knew that with this first adventure we were headed out on a wonderful, new phase in life.

Saturday morning Chris and I began our preparations. We chose our best clothes to wash and iron. With the help of the radio, we practiced singing hymns. We memorized Bible verses.

We scrubbed the house, and did all the things we normally left for Sunday. There would be no time for chores tomorrow!

After lunch, Chris said, "Don't forget to call the church and find out what time we need to be there. We'll have to get up really early. Right, Mom?"

The reminder caught me by surprise. Instead of answering him, I froze. My voice caught in immediate panic.

Call the church! Oh no! I can't remember the name of Norm's church. Oh, Connie, how can you be so stupid. Why didn't you write it down yesterday? Oh no, now what?

I looked at Chris's precious little face so full of anticipation. "Yep, Sweetheart, I will. Thanks for the reminder," I lied as convincingly as possible.

"Now go and play for a little while. After I find the phone number, I'll let you know what they say."

Watching my son take off toward his toys, I put my head down on the table and cried in despair. I couldn't help myself. That little setback felt like a giant disaster.

No matter how hard I tried, I couldn't think of the church's name. All I could remember was that it was close enough for walking.

How would I tell Christopher? I can't disappoint him like this.

The old panic started to build. I heard Chris at the front door talking to someone — probably one of his friends — but I didn't pay much attention. I couldn't move. I had to concentrate.

Think, Connie. Please, God, help me remember! Please!

I heard the door shut and listened to Chris approaching. Hurriedly, I tried to collect myself and wipe the tears off my face.

Before I could look up, Chris ran through the kitchen and tossed a paper down on the table in front me.

"Here, Mom," Chris sang, "the lady said for me to give this to you."

Glancing down at Chris's delivery, I couldn't believe my eyes. EMMANUEL REFORMED CHURCH. It was a church bulletin!

That's it! Thank you, Jesus!
Prayer number two — Answered.

I jumped up and flew after him with excited questions, "What lady, Chris? Where did you get this?"

He looked surprised at my flurry, and answered matter-of-factly, "There was a lady at the door with two little girls. She gave it to me, Mom. She invited us to her church too. But I told her we were already going somewhere else!"

When I heard those words, I ran out the door in search of my miracle lady and children. There they were — across the street, just getting into their car.

Swinging my arms in the air, I hurried to catch them. "Hi," I hollered, "Stop. Don't go!"

They stopped and three astonished faces looked back at me. I didn't care how foolish I looked or sounded. This was a miracle. I wanted to tell them.

"Thanks so much for this," I cried out, waving the bulletin, "you have no idea how important this is to us."

Encouraged by her smile, I continued, "If you've got some time, would you come in for a visit? I really want to tell you what's just happened...what you've done to answer my prayers. Please?"

Without hesitation, my new friends agreed.

As we sat in my front room, I repeated the whole story. I told them how I had just found Christ...how important this first time at church was for us...and how my faulty memory had threatened to stop us.

I didn't quit talking until every detail had been recalled — every detail except any explanation about Bill, of course. I didn't even halt long enough to consider how silly I might sound to them. I didn't care. This was another miracle, and I was overjoyed!

By the time I stopped long enough to focus on anything but my story, I was amazed to see this woman staring at me with almost as much enthusiasm as mine. She looked like an angel to me. Her smile was radiant...knowing...peaceful.

"I understand," she said quietly. "It *is* the most wonderful feeling in the world to know that God hears our prayers. I'm just glad that this time, He used me to help."

"By the way, my name is Mary," she continued. "When you get to church tomorrow morning, look for me. I always go a little early, and I'll wait for you right inside the front entrance. Then after church I'll introduce you to some other people there."

I gratefully accepted her offer and promised to follow her suggestions.

As Mary prepared to leave, it suddenly occurred to me how really unusual it was for me to be a part of this interchange. There I was talking with a stranger about going to church! Just two weeks earlier, I would have laughed at the prospect. I would have said that it could never happen.

Miracle after miracle!

After Mary left, Chris and I busily went about enjoying our happy day. We were having so much fun, neither of us heard Bill's car pull into the driveway.

My first alert of my husband's homecoming was hearing an echo of Christopher's not-too-enthusiastic greeting, "Oh! 'Hi' Dad."

I was in the bedroom, and stopped dead in my tracks. I quit breathing, trying to hear a response from Bill. I could judge his mood as soon as I heard his voice.

But, except for the sound of Chris's feet rapidly approaching my room, there was only silence. That was warning enough!

Chris didn't stop running until he was right in front of me. He looked frightened, like something terrible was about to happen.

Lowering his voice to the tiniest of whispers he asked the questions that I can still hear today. "Mom, is Dad going to hit you again? Will he say we can't go to church?"

In that instant, looking into my child's eyes, nothing else mattered to me. I didn't care where Bill was, or even if he could hear what I was about to say. My fear of him, and what he might do, simply vanished.

I bent down and held Christopher as close to me as I could. And then in a clear, calm voice I gave him the answers he so much wanted to hear.

"No, Honey, Dad isn't going to hit me. He's not going to hit you. And he won't stop us from going to church either. Our plans haven't changed. You'll see. Don't worry. I love you."

As I sat cradling Christopher tightly in my arms, I could feel the relief running through his body. I prayed.

Forgive me, Jesus. It's because of my mistakes that Chris knows fear like this. Stay with me now. Make me strong. Help me find a better way for him. My son deserves so much better.

When I looked up, Bill was staring at us from the bedroom doorway. I didn't know how long he'd been there. I didn't know what he'd heard. I couldn't read his expression, and didn't care to.

"What's this all about?" he asked abruptly. "Exactly what in hell am I *not* going to do?"

"Well, Bill, I told Christopher that just because you're home now doesn't mean that we can't go to church tomorrow like we've planned. And I also said that you're *not* going to get mad and start hitting us either."

I couldn't believe I was hearing my own voice. Where was this courage coming from?

Connie, have you lost your mind? You know how unpredictable this man is. What in god's name are you doing?

I don't think Bill could believe my new attitude either. The expressions on his face revealed a whole gambit of surprised emotions — from stunned confusion to absolute fury...from complete astonishment and rage to a beaten resolve.

A deafening silence lasted for a moment as Bill fought to regain composure.

And then, as if to bolster himself a bit, he said, "I don't give a s--- what you do tomorrow, or any other day, for that matter. Just don't plan on driving anywhere. I've got plans of my own, so the car's off limits."

"That's okay. We'd already planned on walking," I replied confidently. "A lady stopped by this afternoon. She said that the service is at 10:00 a.m., so we'll have plenty of time. She's going to wait by the main entrance for us."

Sensing my strength marked the final blow. This time, there was no attempt to hide the surprise as Bill marched toward Chris and me — his eyes glaring and fists clenched.

"Oh, so now you've got some friends too, huh?" Bill yelled. "Well, little *miss Christian,* you'd better think twice about that if you know what's good for you! You stupid b----, who have you been talking to? What did you say about me?"

The brief seconds that followed seemed to last for hours. All my senses were on alert. I could feel a battle raging inside me — the old, familiar fear was beginning to overpower my will to stay calm.

Bill was standing within inches of where I sat, still holding Chris. At first, I was silent in the face of my attacker. Silently, fervently I prayed.

This is it, Jesus. Help me. What should I say?

Finally the words came. Looking him straight in the eyes, I said, "Bill, I *am* a Christian now — and that changes everything. I know Jesus loves me...He's forgiven my mistakes...He's wiped the slate clean."

"God's given me the chance to start over again, and at Church I can find out how. That's why I want to go...that's the *only* reason."

"I don't want to talk to anyone about you...I haven't...and I won't."

Taking a step back, Bill laughed and replied, "Fine, Connie, do what you want. You've either lost what was *left* of you mind, or you're so dumb it doesn't matter anyway. Just keep your d--- mouth shut!"

With this final decree, Bill turned and stomped off down the hall toward the living room, and parked himself in front of the television. I guess he fell asleep because he didn't move for the rest of the evening. At any rate, relieved that we'd circumvented a fight and not wanting to risk another, Chris and I made a promise to avoid going anywhere near him.

Sunday morning proved to be everything Chris and I dreamed it would be — and more! I kept thinking how lucky we were that God had chosen this church just for us.

It felt perfect. Christ's presence surrounded me. His Spirit filled the place...and marked the faces of His people.

Here *I've found real love, joy, and wisdom. It is wonderful and amazing. Thank you, Jesus.*

Just as she promised, Mary was waiting when Chris and I arrived. There she was, my angel from heaven, smiling and waving us in.

And, standing around Mary, there were others ready to meet us. Their faces were full of expectation. Their voices rang with excited greetings, laughter, and joy.

They put their arms around us and made us feel so loved and wanted. Every bit of hesitancy I had felt until then vanished.

Yes! I belong here. This is my first touch of heaven.

The service was beautiful. Oh, we didn't know what was happening all of the time, but it didn't seem to matter. Chris and I anxiously did our best to follow along.

We sang hymns in our best, practiced voices — all the while pretending to know words and melodies we'd never heard before. We listened to the choir appreciatively and patiently, wondering when it would be our turn to sing again. We listened attentively to the sermon. We fumbled with our Bible, trying to find the right selections. We prayed.

I cried and cried. My heart was filled with pure joy.

When the service was over, Mary said that she wanted me to meet Rev. Bill Miedema, the church's pastor. When discovering her intentions, I was more than a little leery.

My assumption was that no matter their title — ministers, pastors, priests, fathers, whatever — these were somebodies who had a more direct line to the almighty, and lived a notch closer to heaven than the rest of us normal folk. I wasn't at all prepared for any sort of "confessional."

Hearing my protest, Mary laughed. "Don't be silly. We're all brothers and sisters in God's family here...all doing what we can to support each other...and that *includes* our pastor."

"After I left your house yesterday, I told Rev. Miedema about your answered prayer, and he's just as thrilled as we are. Come on, he's been looking forward to meeting you."

Mary was right. As soon as I saw Bill Miedema, I could tell that he was a kind, gentle man. There weren't any hidden agendas. There was no attempt to pry or scold.

"Aha, so here you are. You must be Chris and Connie," the pastor said, grinning from ear to ear, "I'm so happy God helped us find you! It's wonderful to meet you — a miracle for sure! Did you enjoy our service?"

"Yes, more than you'll ever know," I replied, still feeling a bit intimidated. "If it's all right, we'd like to come *every* Sunday."

The pastor laughed and put his hand on my shoulder, *"If it's all right? Of course it's all right!* We couldn't get along without you!"

"In fact, why don't you phone me at the church office tomorrow and we can find a time for the two of us to talk. We'll find just the best spot for you here. Okay?"

"Okay, thank you," I agreed, wondering how on earth I would really manage that.

Glancing around, I noticed that the church's foyer was practically empty, and was reminded that Chris and I had to leave too — and quickly. We still had a long walk home, and Bill was probably already wondering where we were.

For sure. Bill's furious by now.

After thanking Mary one last time, Chris and I headed for home. All the way we talked about our morning, trying to memorize every detail. It was a beautiful spring day, and we were having such a good time recalling what we'd seen and heard, we almost forget to worry about what might be waiting for us when we got home.

But, when we opened the door, our smiles faded. My assumption was accurate. Bill *was* furious.

I didn't even get the door closed before Bill was screaming obscenities and questions.

"Godd--- it woman! Can't you find anything to do besides screw up my life? I've been waiting for hours. Where in the hell have you been?"

Not waiting for an answer he continued, "I suppose you found goody-two-shoes Norm there, huh? So...what did you tell him about us? Did my little slut of a wife do some nuzzling up? Did you get any, you f------ whore?"

I'd heard words and accusations like these a hundred times before. But that morning, they sounded so vile and filthy.

What an incredible contrast between the loving Spirit of God and the evil spirit of this man.

"Bill, don't be ridiculous," I answered firmly. "I've already *told you why we're* going to church. Norm wasn't even there. And it took longer because we had to walk both ways."

"Yeah, right," Bill continued sarcastically, "I know why you're so hell-bent on being seen at that d--- church. You're trying to get me in trouble so you can take off with someone else. But, let me tell you something right now — I'm clean, so keep your trap shut. Besides nobody would want *you* anyway."

All this time I watched Bill more closely than I listened, and unconsciously prepared for the worst. Christopher was tucked safely behind me...my feet were firmly planted...and my arms were free and poised to cover my face at the first blow. So, I was incredibly relieved to see him reaching for his coat and car keys instead of me.

Bill pushed past me to leave. "Uh uh, Missy, no more," he growled. "It won't work. From now on, I'm going *with* you. I can't trust you on your own, so I'll just have to follow along and stomach whatever bulls--- happens at your new 'Sunday school'!"

With a big grin, Bill slammed the door shut behind him.

"See you next Sunday, little miss Christian'!"

Finally, the ranting and raving ended. But it wasn't much of a comfort because I knew this was no idle threat. And what's more, I knew Bill could actually pull it off. I'd seen him do it before.

Oh yes, Bill was very capable of following Chris and me into church and pretending to be a devout worshiper... a perfect gentleman... a loving father and husband.

I felt sick.

Jesus, I love our new church. I want to have it for myself. I want to learn and worship there. I want to feel your love.

How can I do that under such false pretenses?

I'll never know why, but God allowed Bill to keep his awful promise. Practically every Sunday morning for the remainder of that year — almost ten months — Bill looked like the epitome of a loving family man.

He sat close and put his arm around me or held my hand. If I tried to edge away, Bill wouldn't let me move. It was an invisible, but undeniable, command to "put up *and* shut up."

And what a wonderful, congenial personality! Bill was so friendly, he had the entire congregation convinced that he was some kind of saint! Sunday mornings, we were the perfect, happy family.

But Sunday night — under the cover of darkness — the saint turned back into a monster. He made a regular practice of pinning me against a wall and slugging me in the arms, and stomach, and back. Or sometimes he preferred to cover my face with his hands, and bang my head back and forth against the wall.

But, no matter the choice of tactics, when his arms grew tired of throwing blows, Bill almost always forced me to have sex with him.

It made me sick. I felt filthy...wretched...and ashamed.

I begged God to show me a way out. I prayed for understanding. I searched the Bible. I waited for answers.

Encouragement came in a variety of ways. Sometimes it was a Bible verse...the words to a song...a sympathetic call from Norm...a smile from my precious son...a visit from Keely or Kim. There was pain, but there was also peace.

Even though at the time I couldn't understand *why* God allowed my pain to continue, I never felt abandoned. My heart was filled with the Holy Spirit who reminded me each and every day that I was a child of God. Somewhere, somehow Jesus would reveal His plan for me.

false confidence

No one, but Chris and I, had the slightest inkling that we were in real trouble. I remember thinking it was very important to keep my ugly burden buried from view. I was so ashamed, and I honestly figured that no one would understand. It was difficult to do, but I learned to lie like a champ — to my daughters, to my neighbors, to Norm, to my friends at church.

It was a long year. Each morning I woke up wondering if today was *the* day. Each night I mustered new hope for tomorrow.

Then, finally, something happened that made me think my rescue was soon coming.

It was a Friday evening in early December, when I heard a car pull into the drive. Looking out the front window, I was surprised to see not just one, but two police cars parked out front, and four officers starting their approach to the house. I beat the officers to the door, and watched anxiously as they walked up the front steps.

I'm certain I presented a ridiculous source of confusion for these law enforcers. Instead of the worried greeting they were most accustomed to, here was a woman looking as though she was excited to hear their news!

And I was excited! I was convinced they had caught Bill doing something illegal, and that they were here to collect him...confine him...send him out of the country... just anything that would keep him away from me forever!

"Good evening, Ma'am," one officer said, looking at me rather strangely. "We're sorry to bother you, and we don't want to alarm you. Are you Mrs. Sharp?"

"Yes, Sir," I replied. "What is it?"

An officer responded quickly and to the point, "We need to speak with your husband. Is he here, or do you know his whereabouts?"

I was elated.

But gathering my senses, I gave the impression of concern. "Oh, thank goodness one of my girls hasn't been in an accident," I replied as convincingly as possible.

"But, as for Bill," I went on slowly, "he's *not* here. In fact, he hasn't really *lived* in this house for quite a while now."

Oh, could I tell you some stories. If you only knew!

The policemen exchanged quick glances before their leader continued. "Well, Ma'am, it's very important that we find your husband as soon as possible. He's been charged with a felony — writing bad checks to be specific."

"Now, please understand that we don't want to pry into your personal business, but we do have to ask if you have *any* information that could lead us in his direction?"

This is it! Finally. Yes, I'll help you find the scoundrel! You can be sure of that.

Lets see...today's Friday. Bill's sure to come home tomorrow. He hasn't missed a Sunday yet!

I nodded in response — trying to appear worried and indecisive. Then I asked the officers if they would come inside the house to talk, and they agreed.

Standing in the front hall, they waited for my lead. I hesitated for a second and then I began my explanation. It was a perfect plan!

"I was afraid of something like this," I lied.

"But, I really don't know where Bill is right now," I said honestly. "I don't *dare* ask him what he does during the day — or where he stays at night. And the real truth is, I'm past the point of caring."

I could see exasperation written all over the faces of my guests, so I knew I'd better get to the point quickly.

"Bill doesn't call. The last I spoke with him was last weekend. Saturday...that's the only time he shows up here...probably to see if we're still alive!"

"So, I guess if you want to stop by again tomorrow afternoon, he might be here. That's the only suggestion I've got to offer. Sorry!"

Searching the faces of the police officers, I wondered if they were wise to my scheme. If they were, they didn't show it. They just tipped their hats, thanked me for the information, and left.

I woke the next morning full of anticipation. Normally, I dreaded Saturdays, but this day would be different.

I had no idea *how different.*

The morning hours seemed to drag by. I kept glancing out the window, waiting for Bill to show up; and, at the same time, hoping to see an occasional police car drive by, or an unfamiliar vehicle parked at a nearby curb.

Nothing. Nothing.

Be patient, Connie. This will work. Think about something else before you jump right out of your own skin! You can do this...you have to.

It was almost two o'clock in the afternoon when I heard the sounds that, any other day, I would have dreaded most in the whole world. Bill's car was stopped in the drive!

Settle down. Be calm. Act normal. He can't think anything weird is going on here.

Quickly, I grabbed a dust cloth and furniture polish from under the sink, ran to the nearest wood table, and began dusting with what looked like total disregard for whoever might walk into the room.

This is good. I always clean on Saturdays. He won't think anything of this. Just try not to look out the window.

Bill walked into the living room, glanced at me, threw his coat over the couch, and stomped off toward the kitchen. I thought he looked uneasy... agitated...preoccupied.

Does *he know something's up?*

But I wasn't about to ask! I just kept dusting. And I waited.

"Don't you ever buy anything at the d--- grocery store besides bread and lettuce?" Bill hollered with his head stuck into an admittedly bare refrigerator.

"Who can eat this s---, anyway?"

I pretended not to hear. Bad choice!

Bill raged back into the living room swinging a half-empty bag of bread in a clenched fist, and obviously looking for a fight.

"I already know you're the ugliest and dumbest b---- I've ever seen, but are you *deaf* too? Can't you hear me? I'm trying to find something to eat for c----- sake. Doesn't anybody in this f------ house ever get hungry?"

I stood up from dusting the coffee table, and turned around to face Bill. I intuitively braced myself for the blows I figured were inescapable.

All of a sudden, everything seemed to freeze in midair. The screaming stopped. Bill's arms feel down limp to his sides. His expression turned from anger to disbelief.

He stood perfectly still. He looked as if he were staring into space at something behind me.

The window. He sees something outside.

I whirled around to follow his glance, and practically screamed out loud in delight. They were back. The police had followed my lead, and they were finally here to take this devil out of my life once and for all.

Good for you, Connie! You did it all by yourself. Brave girl. Now, that's using your head.

I turned back toward Bill hoping to see some fear in *his* face for a change. But what I saw there literally took my breath away.

Instead of following the police activities outside, as one might expect, his eyes were focused directly at me! It was a stone-cold glare.

"You'll pay for this," he growled so low I could barely hear. "You'll pay."

All I could feel was absolute panic. I was so frightened I had to will myself to move.

Looking back out the window, I could see that two of the officers were almost next to the front steps, and two more were standing by the back door.

No, not this time! Uh, uh, now it's your turn to pay. You won't get away with this anymore. They've got you! I've made sure of that.

Without a word, I ran out of the room, leaving Bill alone to confront his accusers. I headed straight for Chris in his bedroom, and shut the door behind me.

I didn't care about hearing anything. I didn't want to know anything, I only wanted Bill gone!

And in just a matter of minutes he was.

I recall feeling a little surprised not to hear any argument or protest. But at that moment, I didn't care...willingly, or not, he left us alone at last.

My first response was complete relief...unabashed joy. I was so proud of *myself.*

Without any help from anybody, I figured it out and engineered our rescue perfectly!

But in spite of the thrill, I tried to temper by excitement for Chris's sake. I certainly didn't want to make a celebration out of the fact that his father had just been summoned by officers of the law!

I was tempted to dance around the house, and collect everything I could find that belonged to Bill, throw it in the fireplace, and burn it. But instead, I stayed in Chris's room, watched him play, and acted like nothing out-of-the-norm had happened.

It really didn't matter to him that my mind was a million miles away. Chris just loved to have me sit close by. So there I sat, thinking... thinking.

Very, very slowly my joy started to fade. Something didn't feel right. Maybe it was the pure hatred in Bill's last words that reverberated in my head. Maybe it was the surprise that he left without a fight.

I couldn't describe why, but the longer I thought about our brilliant escape, the more anxious and fearful I became. No matter how hard I tried, I couldn't shake the lingering sense that something was very, very wrong.

Don't be silly, Connie. You were spectacular. Your plan worked perfectly. Bill's gone!

And then, with a black, terrifying flash, I knew the truth. Bill didn't put up a fight because somehow he knew the police had no proof.

They can't hold him without proof. And Bill's certainly not going to confess.

He's coming back...and when he does...I'm dead.

Oh, no! Connie, what have you done? Why did you think you could do this all alone?

Why didn't you wait for God...what happened to your faith?

I looked at my watch. Two hours had already passed.

Oh, God, there's not a second to waste! I have to get Chris out of this house and far away. Now!

But where do I go. And how do I get there?

Wait...Bill's car is still here. That's it! I'll take the car somewhere.

Poor little Christopher didn't know why we were in such a rush. But with one serious look at me, he knew not to dawdle.

"Come on, Chris, get your coat on, NOW!" I screamed, quickly losing all self control. "We've got to go."

With our coats still flying open, I grabbed Chris's hand and we practically flew out the front door.

But we were too late! Bill was already at the curb, climbing out of the back of a police car.

Bill looked toward the house and saw us stopped in mid-flight on the steps. He grinned knowingly, and waved.

My heart sank. Terror filled my soul. I couldn't think. I couldn't move.

The details of what occurred during the following hours are too painful...too terrible for me to think about for any length of time.

I managed to get Christopher back into his room, and told him not to unlock the door for any reason, until I said he could. I remember praying for him.

I wondered if either of us would live through the night.

But, in reality, I don't think Bill remembered that little Chris even existed. It was *me* he wanted.

By the time Bill reached the house, he was *completely* obsessed with rage. I truly believe that he was "out of his mind" with anger. He was a demon.

Unless you've seen firsthand this degree of anger, it's difficult to envision how it looks. But for those who have...it's a sight never forgotten!

Bill didn't even resemble the same man! His eyes were glazed... blank...unfocused. The color drained from his face. His features were contorted almost beyond recognition. He made no sound of any kind.

Bill appeared to be totally out of control — and in control at the same time. There seemed to be no limits. He couldn't stop himself, yet each movement was calculated.

He couldn't *be* stopped. No person on earth would have even tried.

What I experienced that night was violence so furious it can only be described as "inhuman" in its strength and persistence.

I was dragged by my hair though the house. I was thrown against walls and windows. I was kicked and beaten relentlessly.

I was raped time after time.

And, when he was done, he left.

I don't want to remember all that went through my terrified mind that night. But I do remember repeating one thought to myself over and over again...

God in heaven, only You can save me from this hell!

in the arms of Jesus

I'll never know how I lived through that final night of abuse. But I did.be

I woke the next morning with a battered body and broken spirit. I could hardly see. I could barely walk. I couldn't talk.

Slowly, I made my way to Chris's room where he was still sleeping. He looked so peaceful...so pure.

Thank goodness for little favors!

Sitting on the edge of Chris's bed, I stared at the wall and felt empty. I couldn't focus on anything but the pain that racked my body and mind.

There were no thoughts about what to do next...no schemes for a brighter future...no hope.

My spirit was broken beyond repair. There was nothing left to do. My efforts were useless.

Jesus, why did you let this happen? You promised to love and protect us. I believed.

Leaving Chris undisturbed I wandered into the kitchen and sank into a chair. I was fighting to stay in control...searching for a glimpse of sanity. The room looked like a battle zone, and visions of the night before flashed through my mind's eye with terrible clarity.

I closed my eyes tight against the horror around me and pleaded with Heaven for answers.

Where are you now, God? I can't go on. I can't do this anymore. Is this it? There really is no hope?

Suddenly, I realized that I wasn't alone. I was with Jesus!

Every fiber of my being sensed His presence.

I could *feel* the wonderful comfort of His loving arms wrapped around me. I could feel the warmth of soft breezes touching my face.

The brightest, most beautiful light I had ever seen surrounded Him, and filled the space where we sat together. It was an extraordinary brilliance that encompassed everything...that seemed to radiate from an unseen, eternal source — with no beginning or end.

I could *hear* a majestic and mysterious kind of "music" resonating through the air. It was a beautiful, clear harmony of sounds that seemed to cascade through the air from far, far away. It was as though a thousand angles were being accompanied by the whimsical and powerful instruments of nature — gentle breezes...lapping rivers... and roaring waterfalls.

And through all of this beauty, I heard the words Christ spoke to me. My Lord said...

"Connie, you are my *child*. I have been loving you...caring for you...protecting you...and preparing a place for you for a long, long time — even before *you* chose to believe in My love.

I have not, and will not forsake you. I am here with you now, and I always will be here. My Spirit has found a home in your heart, my child. It will not depart from you.

You are mine, just as the whole world is mine. Do not be afraid. Believe in Me. Rely on Me, not yourself.

I know you are hurting. I know this isn't easy. But there is a purpose here.

Use your faith in Me as an armor against the evil that threatens. I will be your guide.

Be still, now. And know that I am God."

Peace...an overwhelming, indescribable sense of confidence in God's love flooded my mind, my soul, and body. The turmoil...the fear...the despair was gone.

I opened my eyes and rejoiced!

There is a purpose. Everything is not in vain.

Yes, I have a guardian. Have faith, Connie, and know your God. Wait for Him. Listen.

That day, for just a brief time, I was allowed a glimpse of heaven. I was allowed to feel the arms of Christ surround me.

It was the healing touch of grace I needed during the saddest, most desperate minutes of my life. My moments with Jesus instilled in me an unforgettable respect for God's power and magnificence... His unlimited wisdom...His ultimate control over all of creation...and the extraordinary depth of His benevolence.

From that day on, I have held firmly to the truth that Jesus Christ lives and that He lives to give me life more abundantly.

answers from heaven

It was the week before Christmas, and I was determined to make it the best ever for Christopher. Bill had not been home since that terrible night.

I knew better than to hope he'd never show up again. Yet, every day he was absent, I grew stronger...less frightened...and more determined than ever to follow God's lead in finding a way out.

I put out my "fleece" before God. I gave my word to be patient... if He would just hurry! I figured that was a reasonable trade.

Okay, Lord Jesus, I'll wait for your direction. We can do this Your way. But, please, don't wait too long! Every day I feel like I'm headed a little closer to disaster. I don't think I can live through it again.

How about year-end, Jesus? Could you give me some sign...some instruction by January 1? I know it's a lot to ask in such a short time. But, Lord, I just don't have much time left!

I must have prayed those words a thousand times. And with every session, I grew more confident.

I waited — not knowing for what. I just waited.

Finally my answers came. God revealed His plan for me — and just in time!

Christopher and I had a wonderful Christmas. It was, after all, the very first time we really celebrated Jesus's birth. There were no unexpected interruptions. We were safe and happy.

The evening after Christmas day, while Chris and I were eating dinner, there was a knock at the door. Answering it, I couldn't believe my eyes. It was my sister, Shirley.

She looked like messenger from heaven to me as she stood grinning and reaching for an embrace. I squealed with joy and hugged her with all my might.

"What on earth are you doing here?" I asked. "I'm so glad to see you. Come on in!"

Shirley answered, laughing at my excitement, "Well, I haven't heard from you for so long. To be perfectly frank, I started to wonder if something was wrong. I knew you probably wouldn't tell me the truth over the phone, so I decided to drive across the state and check things out in person — so here I am!"

My eyes filled with tears of joy and regret alike. Instantly, I knew I should have confided in her, but I had felt so ashamed and guilty. I turned away from her and cried.

Studying my reaction, Shirley knew at once that there were troubles. Without asking for any explanations she wrapped her arms around my neck and whispered, "Stop now, Connie. Whatever it is, I'll help. Everything will be all right now."

And then my sister continued with words that simply stunned me. She said, "Connie, I'm a Christian now, and even though you may not believe this, Christ has told me that you needed my help. And that's really why I'm here. No matter what is happening, God will help us work it out. You'll see."

I was so surprised to hear Shirley's message, I pulled away from her and just stared in disbelief.

Shirley believes in Jesus too? This is incredible. Jesus, you're using my own sister? Thank you...thank you.

For the next several hours we talked. I told Shirley everything — about Bill, the abuse, the drugs, the lack of money, my despair. And I told her about *my* new faith in Jesus Christ. We cried together... we laughed...and we prayed.

It felt so wonderful to have her with me and to know that she loved me. It felt wonderful to rid myself of the lies and pretenses.

I didn't want Shirley to ever leave. I knew that as long as she stayed, Chris and I would be safe.

When I pleaded with her not to go home, she smiled. But shaking her head, Shirley responded, "No, Connie, I can't stay. I've got to get back."

"But, I have a plan," she continued with renewed enthusiasm. "The day after New Year, I'll have some money that I can send to you. I'll get it in the mail that same day."

And then, very firmly, Shirley unveiled my first instruction.

"Meanwhile," she explained, "you call someone from your church and see if you can find the name of good, Christian attorney in town. And make an appointment as soon as possible!"

"Now listen carefully, Connie," Shirley went on, "the money I'm sending is for you to put toward paying for a divorce, *first*. Then, if there's any left over, do whatever else you need to do. But first things first. Do you promise?"

"I promise," was my quick reply. But I was stunned.

A divorce? People in my church don't "believe" in divorce. They'll think I'm terrible ...especially since no one has the slightest idea that I'm married to a monster!

Shirley read my mind immediately. And, like sisters are apt to do, she offered more advice.

"Listen to me, Connie! No one in their right mind, for any reason under God's heaven, would tell you to stay in a situation where your very life is in danger.

"Don't be afraid of what anyone else thinks or doesn't think... Christian or not. Jesus Christ is your Father now, and I will never believe that He expects you and Christopher to live like this...in such fear!"

"If it will make you feel better," Shirley continued, "then go ahead and tell them the truth about Bill. Make them understand if you want to. Do whatever you have to. But promise me again that you'll make an appointment as soon as you can, and that you'll follow through with this."

"I will. I will!" I said, shamed by her scolding.

"Okay, then," Shirley replied as she began to leave. "Look for my check by the middle of next week. By that time you should have an appointment already made."

"I'll call you, Connie," Shirley hollered as she left. "I love you!"

"Bye!" I yelled back, "thank you. I love you too."

And, with a wave of her hand, she was gone.

I suppose that no matter how much faith one has, when prayers are actually answered, there is a brief second of delighted surprise. That was certainly true for me that night.

I remember closing the door and standing perfectly still, wondering for an instant if I'd been dreaming. In just a few short hours, I was given the answers that I knew would turn my life around. And the answers had come from a totally unexpected source.

Well, Connie. Here you go. God has kept His promises.

Now, you must keep yours. Follow His lead. Be brave.

And, I did keep my promise. The very next day I found the name of a reputable attorney, and set an appointment for the following week.

As the date approached, I became more and more anxious. I knew that this was a step in God's plan, but I wanted to see into the future. I wanted a clear picture of how everything would work out. I needed reassurance.

No matter how hard I tried to project the details of what would happen, too many questions remained. I prayed for guarantees, but always reached the same conclusion on my own.

Belief in things you cannot see is the real meaning of "faith." Put all your trust in the Lord, Connie. He is in control.

The big day finally came, and everything was ready. Keely came to drive me to the law office and watch Chris until I was finished. The check from Shirley had arrived two days earlier. I had collected all the necessary paperwork.

Everything was ready except for me. I was a nervous wreck.

Where is this leading me, Lord? What will happen tomorrow?

The appointment started much better than I anticipated. I relaxed for a bit while we exchanged introductions. And I listened intently as my attorney, Mr. Hess, explained in detail the steps involved in divorce proceedings...the expected costs...and approximate time frames.

Then Mr. Hess asked if I understood the processes he'd described.

"Yes, I think so," I answered.

"Well then, Mrs. Sharp, are you absolutely certain that this is what you want to do?" he probed.

"Yes," I replied again.

Probably a bit frustrated with my cursory responses, Mr. Hess leaned forward and asked the question I had been dreading.

"Would you explain to me the *reason* you are seeking a divorce, Mrs. Sharp?"

Oh darn! I knew this would happen! Why does he need to know? How much should I tell him? Who will he tell?

This is too difficult. Where *do I begin?*

I hesitated for a minute...walked over to look out of a window instead of facing my confronter...took a deep breath... and told the whole story — from beginning to end — without a break.

I didn't allow myself even a glance at Mr. Hess until I finished talking. When I turned back to face his reactions, I was surprised to find a sad, but sympathetic, expression.

"Mrs. Sharp," he began slowly, "I can't really say that I *understand,* because the truth is I've never had to face the terror you lived through."

"But I can say *this* with complete confidence ... I'm in absolute agreement with the laws governing this State that clearly *deny* any person the right to force another into a situation that is threatening to their own well being, or the safety of their children."

"Accordingly," Mr. Hess continued, "You are absolutely *right* to make this choice. We have all the legal grounds to proceed immediately. It can be completed quickly, and without contest."

"If you have time, I can get the paper drawn up today...now... while you wait. Your signature will put the ball in motion. And you can be sure that I will push this case as fast as I can. I am happy to do whatever I can to help a *survivor.*"

A survivor? Yes! That's exactly what I am.

Within a week, the courts located Bill, and served him with divorce papers. He called, wild with anger.

But, to my surprise and great relief, he never came to the house again, until the day he moved out. Not until months later did I discover the reason for his welcomed absence.

Apparently, Bill had again found his way into illegal activities, and was being watched carefully by authorities during the time of our divorce proceedings. For that reason, he avoided confronting us — particularly since physical abuse was a known condition of the divorce request.

But even Bill's best attempts to avoid his just rewards failed him. Soon after our divorce was final, he was found guilty and sentenced to jail.

Occasionally, he called the house and threatened to retaliate. But, after a while, the calls...the threats...the fear stopped.

My family and friends said, "Well, Connie, it's all over. Finally, you can *forget* it ever happened, and move on."

To that, I reply, "Yes, I *will* move on." But the scars that remain on my body and in my soul are deep.

No, I will never forget.

I hear the expressions that are meant to encourage... "Nothing is impossible. Believe you can do it, and you will."

Yet, I wonder who figures it so. Certainly not anyone who walked in *my* shoes!

There was no earthly way for me to break the destructive cycle of my life by myself. I was not strong enough.

Yet I don't stand completely abashed. Finally, I took that giant leap of faith and put myself in God's hands. *And with God, nothing is impossible.* Maybe it was desperation and nothing to be proud of. But I did it. And if I can — anyone can!

Reflections

Am I proud of myself...my past...my *triumphs?*

No. I am *not* a survivor in my own right. My pride and strength rest only in the knowledge that Jesus saved me.

If I could move back the hands of time, would I do things differently?

Absolutely. life is too short to waste even one day.

If I had a magic wand that could make the years of addiction, abuse, and fear disappear — would I use it?

Instantly.

Have my struggles somehow made me a *better person?*

Not a "better person" — just "better prepared" to face life's challenges. At least I know who I am now. Once I didn't care.

Do I have more compassion and empathy for those around me who suffer? A universe full.

Can I claim to have all the answers? Have I learned all the lessons God has to teach me?

Never.

Does telling the saga of my mistakes somehow erase them from my history?

No, the scars always remind me. Jesus has forgiven me, though. And that's enough.

Oh yes, if I could rewrite the story of my life, I would! The characters would be different...the roles reversed...the scenery changed...the painful chapters marked out.

I detest my memories. I am ashamed of my weaknesses. I anguish over my losses.

Recalling the details contained in this book has been the hardest thing I've ever done. Plus, I still shudder at the thought that others might get a glimpse of who I *really* am (or at least was), and render some pretty harsh, but valid judgements.

But, *what was* can't be changed for me. I know and accept that.

Every day I thank my Lord, Jesus Christ for being such a benevolent God...who waited patiently for me to seek His wisdom and healing...and who unconditionally offered His forgiveness.

And in this promise, there's a brighter side. If the lessons I learned can be used to help another, then there *is* a purpose. I cling to the expectation that there is a chance for others to use my sorry example in order to alter *what is* and *what can be* in their own lives.

Christ proved that His promises are not limited to a lucky few. His loving kindness can be found by *anyone* who searches in earnest!

> BUT TO ALL WHO HAVE FAITH IN HIM, HE WILL GIVE THE RIGHT TO BECOME CHILDREN OF GOD. ALL THEY NEED TO DO IS TRUST HIM TO RECEIVE SALVATION. ALL THOSE WHO BELIEVE THIS ARE REBORN, NOT A PHYSICAL REBIRTH, BUT A SPIRITUAL RENEWAL FROM THE WILL OF GOD.
>
> FOR CHRIST BECAME A HUMAN BEING AND LIVED HERE ON EARTH AMONG US AND WAS FULL OF LOVING FORGIVENESS AND TRUTH. AND SOME OF US HAVE SEEN HIS GLORY, THE GOLORY OF THE ONLY SON IN THE HEAVENLY FATHER.

John 1:12 - 14

I know the painful effects of abuse — both self-inflicted and from the hands of another. And, I shake with frustration and anger when I am forced to admit that there are millions of women, right at this moment, suffering in the same tragic trap...desperately looking for *someone to love them.*

If I were heaven's innkeeper, with the power to gather every one into everlasting safekeeping, I would. But, I can't. Only God can.

Jesus, somehow let me spread the message of hope to victims of abuse and addiction...to all those in my path who, for any reason, live with a broken heart and spirit.

Let me be the "crazy Christian" in someone else's life who is ready and able to point the way toward Your love, forgiveness, and salvation.

Allow me to proclaim your promises to others who are so desperately looking for someone to love them ...

GOD SAID, "DON'T BE AFRAID! YOU WON'T LIVE IN SHAME ANY MORE. THE SHAME OF YOUR YOUTH AND THE SORROWS OF YOUR ISOLATION WILL BE FORGOTTEN.

YOUR CREATOR WILL BE YOUR 'HUSBAND' NOW. THE LORD ALMIGHTY IS MY NAME. I AM YOUR REDEEMER, THE HOLY ONE. I AM THE GOD OF ALL THE EARTH. AND I HAVE CALLED YOU BACK FROM YOUR SADNESS.

I HAVE COME TO YOU, A YOUG WIFE ABANDONED BY HER HUSBAND. AND I SAY THAT I WILL CARE FOR YOU WITH EVERLASTING LOVE."

Isaiah 54: 4 -8

Today, I'm free. I'm forgiven. I'm safe. And I have found *someone to love me* forever and ever. What a miracle!

CHRIST SAID, "I WILL SEARCH FOR MY SHEEP UNTILL I FIND THEM, JUST AS A SHEPHERD CARES FOR HIS HERD. I WILL CARE FOR MY CHILDREN AND I WILL DELIVER THEM FROM ALL THE PLACES TO WHICH THEY ARE SCATTERED.

I WILL LEAD THEM TO REST AND PEACE. I WILL SEEK THE LOST, BRING BACK THE SCATTERED, BIND UP THE BROKEN, AND STRENGHTNE THE SICK."

— Ezekiel34: 11-16

appreciation to

my children, Keely, Kimberly, and Christopher
for remaining a constant source of love and inspiration

my persuader, my *crazy Christian,* Mr. Norman DeNooyer
for not letting me forget the value in lessons learned

my writer, Cheryl Simons
for finding words to tell this story. Cheryl has been a gift from Heaven. I will never forget her dedication to this effort, and commitment to help others through it.

my heavenly father, Jesus Christ
to whom I give all praise, honor, and glory for what He has done in my life and continues to do.

today

Connie Sharp resides in Grand Rapids, Michigan, with her son, Christopher, who at this writing, is twenty years old. Keely and Kim live nearby, and have stayed in a close relationship with their mother. Keely is married with three children, and Kim is a newlywed.

Mrs. Sharp owns and operates a registered child care proprietorship that cares for nine youngsters ranging from the age of twelve months to seven years. In fact, in her professional field, Connie is so widely known and well respected, parents are likely to wait for years for their children to be awarded a cherished spot at "Connie's House."

Mrs. Sharp is also a very active supporter of the Domestic Crisis Center in Grand Rapids, Michigan — a short-term shelter that provides protective housing for mothers and their children who are victims of abuse. You could find Connie there nearly every week ... ministering to frightened mothers ... providing food, clothes, and household items she has collected from contributors ... sharing Christmas toys, Easter baskets, and Thanksgiving treats ... and always, always proclaiming the hope available through Jesus Christ.

www.ingramcontent.com/pod-product-compliance
Lightning Source LLC
Chambersburg PA
CBHW061311280526
45784CB00002B/960